WHAT WOULD

THE ROCKEFELLERS DO?

WHAT WOULD
THE ROCKEFELLERS DO?

How the Wealthy Get and Stay That Way—
and How You Can Too

GARRETT GUNDERSON
MICHAEL ISOM

RipWater

Hardcover: 979-8-986-11941-0
eBook: 979-8-986-11943-4

Library of Congress Control Number: 2016932337

Cover design by Teresa Muniz
Book design by Teresa Muniz
Interior images (@Morphart, @Macon, @piai, @4zevar, @Vector Tradition, @EvgeniyBobrov, @Matsabe) used under license from Shutterstock and Adobe Stock.

Printed in the United States of America on acid-free paper

24 25 26 27 28 29 30 31   11 10 9 8 7 6 5 4 3

Second Edition

Table of Contents

NOTE TO READERS   vii

INTRODUCTION   1

Chapters

CHAPTER 1: A Tale of Two Fortunes   7

CHAPTER 2: The Family Legacy Rings
and the Rockefeller Method   13

CHAPTER 3: How We Discovered the Rockefeller Method   23

CHAPTER 4: The Heart of the Rockefeller Method   31

CHAPTER 5: Leverage Living Benefits to Maximize Insurance   43

CHAPTER 6: Turn Small Assets into Big Ones   63

CHAPTER 7: The Most Certain Type of Insurance   77

CHAPTER 8: But Dave Ramsey and Suze Orman Said No!   85

CHAPTER 9: Design Your Plan Properly   105

CHAPTER 10: Find the Money to Fund Your Life and Legacy   113

CHAPTER 11: Maximize Your Financial Efficiency
and Earning Potential   127

CHAPTER 12: Build Your Team to Protect Your Legacy   137

CHAPTER 13: Create Your Lasting Legacy with
a Family Constitution   147

CONCLUSION: The Economic Value of Certainty   157

APPENDIX: How "Buy Term and Invest the Difference"
Stacks Up Against Optimally-Funded Whole Life   165

THE LEGACY BUILDER FREE COURSE   171
END NOTES   173

Note to Readers

The original version of this book, *What Would the Rockefellers Do?*, was published in 2016. It is now in the hands of hundreds of thousands of people, with thousands of amazing reviews on Amazon. We are now called to complete version two for you.

Why an updated version? The core message has not changed, but the economy has. The banking landscape has changed and is even riskier than it was when we wrote the original version of this book. And with all the pandemic-related changes, hikes in interest rates and inflation, and the launch of new technologies, some areas deserve more expansion in support of your legacy journey.

We also want to provide more insight into and resources for the processes of investing in heirs, hosting family retreats, and capturing the critical philosophies, values, and culture of your family. These are all things you can start to do right away, today, by downloading your bonus resources at rockefellersbook.com/legacy.

The narrator of most of this book is me (Garrett). However, Michael adds stories, insights, and resources in special sections throughout. I write, he supplements; he speaks, I supplement. We are a team.

We've also added new illustrations that share the math behind the centerpiece of the Rockefeller Method: properly structured, optimally funded whole life insurance.

WARNING: One reason we chose to publish an updated version of this book is that misinformed product salesmen tout different products and strategies that not only create risk but are also *unlikely to work*. We want to clearly point these out to you. Just because a product is illustrated with higher numbers doesn't mean that risk is taken into consideration. The methods we will teach do not rely on luck or risk. You do not have to chase returns or start with millions of dollars. There is a specific methodology and tools that are crucial to predictable results.

We want to give a special shout-out and thank you to all the financial professionals who bought previous versions of this book to help promote legacy and financial stability for families. We are so grateful to you.

And finally, a shout-out to you, the reader. We commend you for investing in yourself. We applaud you and support your quest to live a life you love—one of prosperity, where you can focus on what matters most and build the legacy you envision.

Introduction

Friday, June 9, 2006, about 6:00 a.m. My landline rings. At first, I'm confused and don't answer. But the ringing persists.

"What?!" I belt into the phone.

I hear the voice of my business partner, Michael Isom. Slowly, shakily, he says, "The company plane left after our event last night, and nobody has heard from Ray or Les."

Umm, what? How? I mean… there has to be some explanation.

Ray and Les are our business partners—and more than that, our friends.

I turn on the TV to breaking news: A plane has crashed into Utah Lake, near the small airport where Ray and Les were supposed to have landed last night.

I'm in shock. My brain doesn't want to accept it.

In a company retreat just a month before, our firm had come up with the idea to work together to write a book. We were excited to get started. The idea was fueled by hearing over and over again at our events, "I wish I would have heard about this sooner!" Or "How do I share this information with my kids, my parents, and my friends?"

But with the unexpected and devastating deaths of our partners and the lessons we still had to learn, it wasn't yet time for *this* book to be written. I hadn't yet met Sheila Brandenberg, a CPA for the Rockefeller Global Family Office. We hadn't yet seen the risks to our partners' legacies after their deaths. It was surprising and alarming to witness people approaching their widows with ideas for how to use their life insurance proceeds. People would request meetings to pitch business ideas, ask for real estate funding, and more. They couldn't afford to chase risky opportunities. Structures and rules with trusts were required to protect and preserve their wealth.

What is a Family Office?

A Family Office is a team of financial professionals—accountants, attorneys, investment advisors, risk managers, etc.—who work together to build your family's finances and legacy under your guidance. The key is, they share your philosophy and work on your behalf, instead of in silos where isolation creates risk, leaks money, and may even result in lack of coordination or conflict.

In 2015, Michael and I were in Las Vegas between Christmas and New Year's Eve, preparing for the next year. *What Would the Rockefellers Do?* was born during our conversations that week, and the original version was published a decade after the plane crash. By that time—with the deaths of our partners, the deaths of clients, and the risks to their families and legacies—we had firsthand experience of what we cover in this book.

As financial advisors, Michael and I have worked with thousands of people in different phases of their lives. It has given us a unique perspective. We have also had access to an amazing research team and attorneys as we explore what works and is most critical for preserving and perpetuating wealth. This book has been designed over decades of deep discussion, hosting workshops, and bringing the concepts to life for our clients.

Michael is instrumental in sharing our message both on the stage around the United States and through one-on-one work with countless clients. He delivers masterful speeches with emotion and engagement, inspiring audiences to live and leave a legacy. It is one thing to read about it, and another to experience it. If you host events or know someone who does, I highly recommend that you get in touch with us at rockefellers-book.com/speaking to book Michael.

Michael has also written a fantastic book titled *What We're Worth: Realize Your HLV (Human Life Value) … and Know What You're Really Worth!* I endorse and highly recommend it as a perfect companion to this book. It's both easy to read and highly impactful. You can check it out at vaultais.com/worth.

Michael and I have known each other for almost a quarter of a century. We met way back in 1999 when I was still in college. Michael had just started in financial services at Guardian Life. We had a relentless curiosity about personal finance and studied it together at the small dining room table in my college apartment. That curiosity was—and still is—one of our key advantages.

In our quest to discover the rules of money used by the wealthy, we flew all over the country every month for twenty-six straight months attending symposiums, masterminds, and other events. We interviewed the best minds in finance and sat in on high-level meetings. This education was instrumental in helping us see through the myriad myths and misinformation that confiscate wealth through confusion and risk.

The success of *What Would the Rockefellers Do?* has been beyond our expectations and an exciting journey to share with our readers. And since we wrote version one, my life has drastically changed. After creating a family mission statement, establishing our family rules, designing our family crest, doing years of regular family meetings, and hosting family retreats, my family is living our legacy. It is often progress over perfection, but the process has been deeply rewarding.

There is more work for my family to do—different work. My sons require support in choosing their careers. I have so much more to teach them about money. I want to encourage them to pursue lifelong learning and live on purpose. However, the foundational information discussed throughout this book has been instrumental in establishing a context for their generational wealth moving forward.

My eldest son, Breck, currently travels with me to speaking engagements. I pay him to support me with setting up book signings, handling the details for the trip, filming me while speaking, editing my speaking footage, and more. He also gets a new form of education that school cannot provide. By listening to my speeches and engaging in conversations with people at events, Breck naturally learns valuable life lessons without being in a classroom. I love being able to have this time with him.

Another way I am living my legacy is by creating a life I don't want to retire from. I sold my business, embraced a new phase of life, and now spend my time doing the things that are aligned with my Soul Purpose. I challenge myself in the most rewarding ways, including by doing comedy, which has been a lifelong dream. I filmed a comedy special and have been on two comedy tours. I even wrote a children's book about money with my co-author, Julia Cook.

What is Soul Purpose?

Soul Purpose is your unique set of talents, abilities, and passions applied productively and effectively making an impact upon the world and bringing the highest levels of joy and fulfilment for you and for those you create value for. Soul Purpose is who you are when you are at your best. When your work is in alignment with your Soul Purpose, you feel more alive, your energy increases, you become more optimistic and there is an excitement for the future.

For more details on how Soul Purpose applies to wealth creation, see my book, *Killing Sacred Cows 2.0*.

My youngest son, Roman, has done stand-up comedy with me. He has opened for me multiple times, including in the special we filmed when he was only thirteen years old. My kids have watched me follow my dreams and struggle to do new things. They have been paid to help me rehearse comedy and the theatrical keynote I developed based on my most recent book, *Money Unmasked*.

One of our greatest accomplishments as a family was in 2017, when we spent the summer in Italy. That summer forever changed our family for the better.

This is all part of living my legacy. And I share it with you not to brag, but because I want to inspire you to live your own version of legacy. That is why I am also sharing the resources that have allowed for all of these things to be possible. To help you implement and personalize what you'll learn in this book, I'm sharing my Legacy Builder course, which includes videos and a workbook. You can get the Legacy Builder course for free at rockefellersbook.com/legacy. You can also share any of those downloads with the people you love as our gift to support your legacy.

THIS IS NOT A HACK!

Our society today loves "hacks" and shortcuts to a better life. The world of personal finance is no different. Product salespeople focus on one product or strategy and tout it as the end-all, be-all financial product.

We want to stress up front that the products and strategies we discuss in this book are not "hacks." They won't help you get rich quickly. They won't solve all of your financial problems. They are not the only things for you to consider, but rather pieces of a more holistic puzzle.

What we present to you here is not a wealth hack. Rather, it is a comprehensive philosophy based on financial principles that have been proven to stand the test of time. It is a production-expanding mindset. It is a holistic, intelligent, coordinated system for maximizing your wealth not only while you're alive, but also long after you've passed.

Those who create wealth—and keep it—demonstrate over and over again that there *are* no hacks that bring lasting wealth. Creating, growing, protecting, and perpetuating wealth is a conscious, deliberate process. It takes vision, perseverance, the right tools and strategies, and a comprehensive team. It requires having a comprehensive plan and executing it diligently.

This book is about what to leave behind and how to leave it behind. But most importantly, it's about what you can do today to change your family's financial future and destiny. Our sincere hope is that this book inspires you to consciously build and live your legacy. We want to teach you how to pass down generational wealth in a way that brings out the best—not the worst—in your heirs. This is possible when you do what the wealthy do.

CHAPTER 1

A Tale of
Two Fortunes

"Only the man who does not need it is fit to inherit wealth—the man who would make his own fortune no matter where he started. If an heir is equal to his money, it serves him: if not, it destroys him. But you look on and cry that money corrupted him. Did it? Or did he corrupt his money?"

—AYN RAND, *Atlas Shrugged*

Imagine one of your great-grandchildren presiding over a family fortune. Imagine her benefiting from it in various ways: supplementing her education; making a down payment on her first home; acquiring a business; navigating financial disasters like illness, medical bills, or disability; or getting a preferred rate of interest on a loan from the trust.

Now imagine that every time she does this, she toasts your memory and the legacy you built for your family. She toasts you because you initiated it all. You were the catalyst. You took a new step, guided your family in a new direction, and made a profound choice to break the chains of generational financial bondage.

You acted consciously, deliberately, and wisely to build wealth. But more than that, you left behind a set of values, rules, and guidelines to shepherd that wealth for generations. And providing for your heirs didn't require you to take massive risks, understand complicated concepts, or sacrifice your life.

You didn't work hard but with the wrong philosophy, only to create spoiled kids and unproductive wealth. You didn't destroy your legacy and force your descendants to start over again and again. Instead, you learned from and did what the wealthy do.

It shouldn't come as a surprise that the wealthy do the opposite of what most people do when it comes to growing, protecting, and perpetuating wealth. After all, there's a reason why they've achieved the results they have!

Many people work hard to become wealthy but never quite make it. What limits their wealth isn't a lack of effort, but rather a lack of financial education. Now that you've found this book, you have a different choice. This is a pivotal moment for you, for your finances, and especially for the people you love most.

You can do more than just leave your kids better off than you were. You can spark a financial legacy of wealth, contribution, and empowerment that lasts for generations. You can create a family fortune that lives on in perpetuity. And you can do it without creating "trust fund babies" who know how to spend money and little else. Instead, your wealth can be used to empower future generations. It can act as a launchpad for all of their endeavors, whether professional, academic, charitable, or entrepreneurial.

Some parts of the method we'll share with you in this book, such as basic structure and implementing financial instruments, are easy. Other parts require more time, attention, and intention. Legacy requires careful planning, it has been done by many others and can be done by you and yours.

THE VANDERBILTS VERSUS THE ROCKEFELLERS

For real-world examples, we need only look to America's past. In the nineteenth and twentieth centuries, two of America's wealthiest businessmen amassed incredible fortunes that each towered over the fortunes of Bill Gates, Warren Buffet, and Mark Zuckerberg. Their names were Cornelius Vanderbilt and John D. Rockefeller. The stories of what happened to their fortunes reveal many lessons for anyone planning to leave wealth for the next generation.

The Fortune of Cornelius Vanderbilt

Cornelius Vanderbilt made his fortune in the transportation business, starting by ferrying goods and passengers around New York Harbor in the late 1820s. Soon, his business expanded to shipping goods from the West Coast to the East Coast, using Nicaragua as a passageway. Eventually, he switched from ships to trains, where he made his largest fortune yet in the railroad business. At his death in 1877, Vanderbilt's fortune was estimated to top $100 million, which was more than the US Treasury held at the time. In today's dollars, that's more than $250 billion (with a "b").

But even as the richest man in America, Vanderbilt lived a relatively modest life. He gave some money to charity—he donated $1 million to help start Vanderbilt University, and he also donated to churches. But 95% of his fortune was passed on to his son, William Henry Vanderbilt, leaving his wife and other children to split the rest.

William Henry Vanderbilt did well, doubling the family fortune before his death nine years after the passing of his father. But that was the last time the Vanderbilt family fortune would grow. The Vanderbilt heirs became known as wealthy socialites with a penchant for lavish spending. There were ten Vanderbilt mansions built in Manhattan, including the largest private residence ever built there, plus several more around the country. Many of these homes seemed more like palaces, such as The Breakers in Newport, Rhode Island, which still stands today.

But with no new money coming in, the fortune couldn't survive the spendthrift Vanderbilt heirs. By 1947, all ten Vanderbilt mansions in Manhattan had been torn down. It is said that Cornelius Vanderbilt's last words were, "Keep the money together." But the Vanderbilt heirs failed fabulously. The family fortune was squandered in just a handful of generations. A direct descendant of Cornelius died broke just forty-eight years after Cornelius died.

The Fortune of John D. Rockefeller

John D. Rockefeller made his fortune selling oil and kerosene. He started Standard Oil of Ohio in 1870. By the end of the decade, his business was refining more than 90% of the oil in the United States. Rockefeller's objective was to deliver the best oil at the cheapest price. He once wrote to a partner, "We must ever remember we are refining oil for the poor man, and he must have it cheap and good."

Rockefeller succeeded spectacularly, pushing the price of oil down from .58 cents to .08 cents a gallon. The result was that Rockefeller became the richest man in American history. The *New York Times* wrote in Rockefeller's 1937 obituary that he had amassed more than $1.5 billion; estimates of his wealth vary between $300 and $400 billion in today's dollars.

Rockefeller was a prolific philanthropist, donating more than $530 million of his fortune to charity during his lifetime. He also left $460 million to his son, John D. Rockefeller Jr. (otherwise known as "Junior"), in 1917. Unlike the Vanderbilts, Junior kept the family money together by creating trusts for each of his six children. The bulk of the family fortune was put into these trusts, which provided Junior's kids with the interest income and were managed by a group of financial professionals referred to as the "Family Office."

Six generations later, a Family Office still manages the Rockefeller fortune, which is estimated to be more than $10 billion. An estimated two hundred Rockefellers currently receive interest income from the family trusts. The family is also said to donate as much as $50 million per year to charity, carrying on the senior Rockefeller's tradition of philanthropy.

CHOOSING THE ROCKEFELLER METHOD

Why did the Rockefellers keep their fortune while the Vanderbilt family lost nearly everything? The answer, ironically, is that the Rockefellers heeded the last words of Cornelius Vanderbilt. They did "keep the money together," using trusts as a legal tool to protect the fortune from taxes, lawsuits, and spendthrift heirs as much as possible. The Rockefellers hosted family retreats, invested in their heirs, and had a financial team (aka Family Office).

This wise financial planning has empowered six generations and counting of Rockefellers. Many Rockefellers have found success in business and politics, with three governors, a senator, and a United States vice president among John D. Rockefeller's descendants.

Conversely, the last well-known Vanderbilt descendant is the television host Anderson Cooper, who had to fight his way into the industry—even forging press credentials—to get a chance to report the news. The Vanderbilt fortune was not there to help him.

The lesson is clear: If you want to empower your children, grandchildren, and great-grandchildren—and beyond—don't simply leave them money to spend as they please. Keep the money together. Design trusts that direct how money can and cannot be spent. And pass your values and vision on to the next generation so they don't stop with you.

The Rockefeller Method isn't just for the Rockefellers. Michael and I have changed our families' financial destiny by using this method and the financial strategy at its core, and we've devoted our lives to helping other families do the same.

CHAPTER 2

How We Discovered the Rockefeller Method

Neither Michael nor I were born into wealth—in fact, just the opposite. Our upbringings gave us both the ambition and drive to learn and do what the wealthy know and do. Each of us has taken a journey to discover the principles, tools, and strategies of the Rockefeller Method.

You have your own story, too. We hope our stories inspire you to continue your efforts to build, grow, and preserve generational wealth and create a new story for your family.

GARRETT'S STORY

I am a coal miner's son. Both of my grandfathers were coal miners. Hell, even my great-grandfather, Biagio Eaquinto, was a coal miner. Yet I have never set foot in a coal mine. My parents imagined something different and better for me. They wanted to create for me a life without undue physical stress and danger, one with more purpose, upside, and fulfillment than they had experienced.

I go bowhunting with my dad every year. During the downtime, I've started documenting my dad's story. I want to know more about his childhood and early life. One thing I've learned about is his regret that he didn't put more effort into school. But instead of being a victim or complaining, he got a college degree while working in the mine full-time. Choosing action over regret, he led by example.

It was certainly a team effort. While he studied, my mom worked full-time, cooked, cleaned, and made sure our homework was done. She enforced boundaries and standards and encouraged me and my siblings to participate in sports, join clubs, get good grades, and sample what life has to offer. That is my parents' legacy.

I am grateful that my ancestors had the foresight and courage to provide a better life for their descendants. It wasn't easy. It was a tough road.

It began in 1913, with a difficult but transformational choice. My great-grandfather, Biagio, was unable to make a living in his hometown of San Giovanni in Fiore, Italy, so he made the courageous—and risky—choice to leave for America. He left his pregnant wife and made a long and arduous journey that eventually terminated in East Carbon, Utah, where he found a job as a goatherd and later as a coal miner. He spent seven long years there, separated from his wife and family, living in a tent. By the time his wife and children joined him, his youngest daughter—whom he had never seen—was seven years old.

Biagio's journey and sacrifice created folklore that was passed down through our family—some of it inspiring, most of it debilitating. We heard stories of hardship, fear, and worry. My great-grandfather did all he could to avoid poverty, only to get stuck in a cycle of scarcity. But his journey was a bold, critical move that would alter the destinies of generations.

His son James, my grandfather, built on Biagio's legacy and took even more steps in the right direction. He, too, was a coal miner, but he also had two side businesses repairing televisions and playing the accordion in a band. As a kid, I often tagged along as he drove his red repair van filled with tools and gadgets or sat and watched him work in his shop. Everyone in our small community knew and respected him. I grew to admire him more and more.

My grandfather is my hero. He was the patriarch who held our family together. He always found and made time for family; he was at every ball game, birthday party, and holiday. His time, attention, and example were also key to freeing our family from the shackles of generational scarcity. It wasn't easy. It required facing decades of fear and choosing a new path. Imagine if he'd had all of that *and* the power of the Rockefeller Method early on.

My grandfather was my first client. When I started out in financial services at nineteen, my family, being the nice, supportive people they are, agreed to let me help them out. I managed some of their money, and as the market rose in 1998 and 1999, their finances grew, too. In my little community, I was initially viewed as a financial Einstein. Initially.

But when the market went down in 2000, I realized that I had been riding a wave. As Warren Buffett said, "After all, you only find out who's swimming naked when the tide goes out." I was definitely swimming naked.

This was one of the most pivotal times of my life. Instead of telling people they were "in it for the long haul," or "the market is on sale," I chose a different path. I faced each of my clients and got them completely out of the declining market between March and May of 2000. This saved them hundreds of thousands of dollars. (It would have been millions if I had been managing more money, but I was in my very early twenties and had fortunately just started.)

I also admitted to them that I didn't know what I was doing. My training at the time was mainly in sales and products, not in markets and strategy, and I came clean with each client about my limited training.

This was difficult for me. I wanted to be seen as a genius, as someone with all the answers. But I had fallen prey to the faulty philosophies perpetuated onto the middle class. The myths that increase risk, limit cash flow, lack accountability, and rarely consider legacy. Things like, "High risk equals high return." "Diversify and dollar-cost-average." "You're in it for the long haul." "Avoid debt like the plague." These "commonplace" ideas are rarely, if ever, practiced by the wealthy. I discuss these money myths in detail in my book, *Killing Sacred Cows 2.0.*

Thankfully, I did the hard thing and kept my clients' trust as I saved them money. I also told them to find another advisor or wait until I figured out what to do—which I did. I immersed myself in financial education for years. Among many other things, I discovered the origins of the Rockefeller Method and how to support the wealthy in protecting, preserving, and passing on their wealth.

During this time, my grandfather's sister—my great-aunt—got really sick and entered the hospital. This concerned my grandfather and his other sister, in part because my great-aunt, who had never married, stored all of the family money in her account—even though two-thirds of it belonged to her siblings.

When she went into the hospital, my grandfather and other great-aunt sat me down and said, "Garrett, we really need your help." No one was just being nice anymore. They desperately wanted to figure out how to use their money to care for my great-aunt and avoid losing it to nursing care expenses and medical care costs.

I came up with a strategy for them to take care of their sister without having the money that was meant for all three of them evaporate in a year or two. This left a deep impression on my grandfather, who rarely spent money on anything other than his grandkids. Some might call him cheap, others frugal. And if my grandfather was frugal, my great-aunt was a miser. She hoarded money in Folger's coffee cans, which she put in the cellar. It is rumored that she applied for welfare even though she had over half a million dollars in her savings account.

My family never talked about money, wealth, or value creation. Their fear and lack of understanding governed their thoughts and actions around money. They weren't taught to be stewards of their money, and therefore all they did was hoard it.

I felt really good about helping my family out, and my family was pretty impressed with me. But a different reality set in when my grandfather asked me, "When you graduate, are you going to get a real job?"

Even after I had helped them with this great financial strategy, my grandfather didn't believe being in business for oneself was a real job because that is what his father had taught him. For my family, it wasn't stable or secure enough. It seemed like a risk and was unfamiliar territory. The trip from Italy to the United States left scars and created generational baggage.

My grandfather and father both belonged to unions that went on strike. I remember my parents eating saltine crackers for weeks at a time because they didn't have money for food while the mining union was on strike. And yet to them, being an entrepreneur seemed risky.

During my senior year, I got more and more sad and frustrated. I couldn't see a clear vision of my future. I had job offers from Arthur Andersen, Merrill Lynch, American Investment Bank, and Strong Investments (the number two mutual fund family in the world at the time). But because of the doubt that had permeated my family for generations, I was constantly questioning whether I should continue with my business or if I should just take one of the job offers.

Even though I was already making money in the financial services field, I almost decided to work for Strong Investments in Milwaukee. My girlfriend at the time, and now wife—my favorite person in the world—advised me, "I don't know if I want to go to Milwaukee, but you should follow your dreams." The problem was, I couldn't tell if that was what I was doing.

Even in school, almost nobody was encouraging me to stay in business—except one professor: the dean of the business school, Carl Templin. In a meeting, Dean Templin said to me, "You're already making more than all of your professors, and you love what you do. Why would you take advice from them about your career? They are here to educate you in other areas. You just keep doing what you're doing."

So I chose to stay in business, even though it wasn't a "real job" according to my family at that time. As it turned out, by helping another one of my professors (who had managed $5 billion in a municipal bond fund before becoming a professor), I ended up making a single commission that was higher than any of the salaries I had been offered.

I showed my grandfather my bank account to let him know that everything was going to be okay. I told him about all the ways I was helping my clients. And then he started telling everyone about my new career. He would constantly put his hand on my shoulder and look me in the eyes, his own eyes welling up with tears, and tell me how proud he was of me. He realized that I was doing what I love to do and that I was changing the future and financial destiny of our family. He realized that I was creating and living a legacy.

The strategy I ended up teaching my grandfather and his sister was the first piece of what became the Rockefeller Method. This knowledge can give you the chance to change your family's financial future so that the next generation isn't born into financial bondage. I started the initial phase of this strategy by moving my money away from the bank and mutual funds to a foolproof, never-fail strategy using trusts and properly structured, optimally funded whole life insurance to store and protect wealth. It has since evolved into something I use to perpetuate my legacy, increase my cash flow, and capitalize on opportunities when they arise.

This methodology allowed my grandparents to leave an extra $250,000 to their heirs tax-free while enjoying a fuller life in their last ten years. That $250,000 may sound small to some, but they lived in a community where houses sold for $20,000 to $40,000. It was nothing short of life-changing for them.

Now, our family can advance instead of starting over every time someone from the previous generation passes away. And I can take what my grandfather wished he could have given me and give that opportunity to future generations.

MICHAEL'S STORY

To give you an idea of how poor we were when I was growing up, I paid my mom rent through my senior year of high school just to help out.

I fell in love with motorcycles in the seventh grade, when I took my first job cleaning them and sweeping floors at Cycle Town Yamaha. My wage started at $2.25 an hour. Each year they paid me more, so by the time I was a senior in high school I was earning $2,000 per month. That's how I paid for motorcycles, clothes, and dating girls.

When I began attending college in 1993, I started selling cell phones. In my first thirty days, I made $20,000—ten times what I'd been earning at the shop! I had never made $20,000 in a year, let alone in thirty days.

In college, I met my beautiful wife, Wendy. We soon had two kids, Kennedy and Kadin. I felt like I was living the American dream, making money and investing.

I found out I was good at it. So I became a financial strategist and formed a company with three partners: Ray Hooper, Les McGuire, and yes, Garrett Gunderson, to help others be successful with their money.

One day, Les came to me and said, "Hey, I have this real estate deal going on with this investor guy. Maybe you want to get in on it? "

I checked it out and it looked good. I trusted Les, so I started with a shoo-in investment of $50,000. Investor Guy started paying me 5% a month. Wow! Every month, I received a check for $2,500. I dropped another $250,000 into the fund. Bigger checks kept coming, so I gave him another $500,000!

I thought, *I bet my client, Joe, would like to get in on this, too.* And Charles. Then Kate.

The next thing I knew, I had $4.8 million of my own money and over $10 million of my clients' money in Investor Guy's deal, and it was paying all of us 5% every month.

Until August of 2007, that is, when the checks didn't arrive. *Huh, that's not good.* September, no checks. Investor Guy had now stopped taking my calls. I was starting to get a really bad feeling.

Over the next four months, I took money out of my own pocket to cover interest payouts to my clients because I didn't want to leave them hanging.

Then I received a phone call. "Hi, this is Special Agent Mark Jones from the FBI. I want to talk to you about your business activities with Investor Guy. "

The next thing I knew, I was signing a deal with the Feds.

But it was too late. The money was all gone. $4.8 million in my family's life savings and $10 million in my clients' money had vanished.

I couldn't keep the company together. I was under constant, terrifying stress while being interviewed by the FBI and having them comb through my financial records. I started drinking. Not just occasionally—I was drinking myself silly every night. I soon added anxiety meds and narcotics to mask the pain. I became a complete asshole to everyone around me. The stress was so unbearable that I started breaking out in hives all over my body.

One morning at 6:00 a.m., I heard a knock at the front door. It was Wendy's family, here to help her and the kids move out.

I was in a state of shock, but I couldn't blame them—I wasn't healthy to be around. Twelve hours later, I was alone on the bathroom floor, hyperventilating and holding a 9 mm Ruger P89 pistol with a bullet in the chamber. I pressed the gun against the roof of my mouth. My hand was shaking. In my mind, I screamed to God, ready to end it all.

Suddenly, I felt a rush through my body like I'd never felt before. I knew I wanted to live. I put the gun down and made a promise to God and myself: I would extract the lessons from this, apply them in my life, and share them with as many people as I could.

That is exactly what I have been doing since the fall of 2010. I sobered up. I called Garrett. We sat down and talked. He advised me, "You can choose to leverage your past experiences moving forward. Choose to produce your way out of this."

It was from these devastating life lessons that the brand and core message of my current company was born: Vault AIS (standing for asset, investment, and strategy). When I lost our family's entire life savings, I felt worthless. I had tied my self-worth to my financial balance sheet. I stopped believing in myself. I stopped growing as a result.

Garrett reminded me of my human life value balance sheet. Just like a financial balance sheet, that balance sheet also has assets and liabilities. Assets include our experiences, education, integrity, morals and values, relationships, etc. Liabilities include limiting beliefs, bad habits, ignorance, poor character, etc.

I share this because no matter where you start, or the mistakes you have made, you deserve to build and leave a legacy.

As we will discuss more throughout this book, human life value is the source and creator of all property value. People are the true assets; material things are not. The formula is simple: If we want to create more property value in our lives, we must first seek to increase our human life value.

I am happy to report that, thanks to partnering with Garrett in 2011, I earned back all the cash that I lost by

What Is "Human Life Value"?

Life insurance companies determine the amount they'll insure you for based on what they call "human life value." Human life value represents your economic value to the world. Think about how much money you make on an annual basis today, and about the services you offer to your clients and the people around you. If you were to die tomorrow, how much value would be taken from the world versus what would remain if you were to live and work for another thirty years? That is your human life value.

mid-2018. And not only the cash; I had my life back. My courage and confidence, line items in the asset column of my human life value balance sheet, returned. Self-care was a big part of that. Creating value for others by sharing the life-saving messages in this book is another.

When I lost all that cash with Investor Guy, I had forgotten that my number one investment is myself. All the cash any of us has ever earned has come from our ability to produce. I regained that clarity and focused on improving my human life value balance sheet, and the dollars followed.

I also moved back in with my family. Wendy and I recently celebrated our thirtieth wedding anniversary. Our daughter Kennedy is married to her sweetheart, Corbin, and they have a beautiful son, Weston, our grandson. Our son Kadin completed a two-year internship in Southern California and is now helping me with his talents in the areas of video, tech, and AI. Kadin and I also share a passion for riding dirt bikes in the deserts of southern Utah.

Wendy and I now strive to be clear on and deliberate about the morals and values we want to pass on to our children, and how to do so using a family legacy trust. It's deeply fulfilling for us to have our financial life structured in this way. Legacy planning like the wealthy do gives us both more purpose behind everything we do. I wake up empowered to create and exchange with others. I love learning the most efficient and productive ways to leverage these financial tools.

What I share with you in this book, I learned the hard way. I hope you learn from my example and my education how to avoid my mistakes and live as the wealthy do.

For our families, we implement the Rockefeller Method—and do everything we can to avoid the Vanderbilt way.

Which path do *you* choose? And how will that choice influence your posterity?

CHAPTER 3

The Family Legacy Rings and the Rockefeller Method

Rockefeller-style planning works regardless of whether you leave $1 million or $100 million behind. If you plan the right way, you can make your financial legacy last in perpetuity. You can pass on more than wealth to the next generation; You can leave them values, opportunities, and empowerment.

The Rockefeller Method is at the center of what we call the "Family Legacy Rings," which are:

1. Family Office

2. Family Retreat

3. Family Constitution

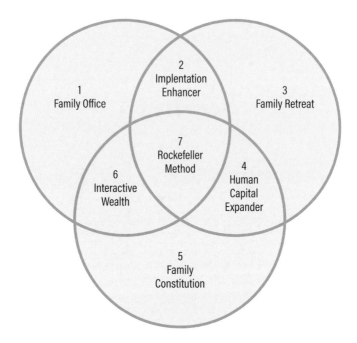

Below we will detail the three Family Rings. For the purposes of this book, we will not cover the Implementation Enhancer, Human Capital Expander, and Interactive Wealth aspects of the Rockefeller Method.

When you utilize this method, you stack the odds in your favor to create a legacy that lasts.

THE FAMILY OFFICE

Steve Jobs, IBM, and many iconic companies attribute their exponential growth and success in business to A-teamers. In finance, the secret sauce is the same. The Rockefellers knew it (six generations strong), but the Vanderbilt family didn't (three generations' money gone). Protecting and perpetuating your wealth requires an integrated A-team.

The Rockefellers had an office of financial professionals—attorneys, accountants, investment advisors, risk managers, etc.— working solely for their family. It would require $300 million or more in net worth to justify such a dedicated team. Thankfully, you can use a fractional or virtual Family Office. This is a financial team that coordinates, communicates, and provides comprehensive financial services for your family as well as others.

It's critical that every member of your Family Office shares the same philosophy and works on your behalf. This is in contrast with the way most people operate their finances, with each advisor working in a silo. Managing your finances in silos creates risk, leaks money, and perpetuates a lack of coordination—and potentially even conflict.

THE FAMILY RETREAT

Building intimate, trusting relationships within your family requires intention, structure, conversation, and living by example. Having regular meetings with agendas, identifying family rules, and creating a structure and rituals are all essential to the perpetuation of non-monetary aspects of legacy. Recurring meetings and retreats allow for a transfer of philosophy and further creation of family traditions, rituals, and insights so that these critical factors can truly come to live in the hearts and minds of your heirs, rather than only on legal documents or solely in your mind. The meetings, rituals, and traditions create space and time for development, buy-in (people support that which they help to build), and refinement of what your family stands for.

In today's world, there are many blended families. Your kids may be grown and out of the house already. Whatever your situation may be, the key is progress over perfection. Rather than host multiple-day events to try and outline your mission and traditions or create your family crest, start small and simple. Find a reason to bring people together in a fun way. Then you can add an hour or two of conversation by asking questions. I've written questions on 3x5 cards for us to use during drive time. Some were just fun, while others were key for deeper thinking and connection.

THE FAMILY CONSTITUTION

The United States Constitution is the oldest active codified constitution in the world. Its 4,543 words have played a crucial role in limiting government and creating freedom.

Your carefully crafted Family Constitution—the preamble to your trust—is designed to do the same for you and your heirs. The purpose of the US Constitution is to protect (not grant) the natural rights of life, liberty, and the pursuit of happiness. A Family Constitution can protect equal rights, not provide equal things. Through proper incentive-based planning, a board of trustees, and an articulated philosophy, your heirs can benefit when they are wise stewards of the resources they are provided. But they are not entitled to anything if they choose to do nothing.

THE ROCKEFELLER METHOD

How can you best mitigate risk and transfer wealth? What if you left a heritage, not just an inheritance?

I believe that the Family Legacy Rings, with the Rockefeller Method at the center and where wealth is centralized and directed by a carefully planned trust, is the best way to perpetuate, preserve, and protect wealth. The Rockefeller Method is a specific trust that owns your specially designed, optimally funded life insurance contract on you and your family members. It includes asset protection and uses trusts to enact your plan to empower your heirs for generations.

If you have a trust, you can keep your assets private, avoid probate, minimize tax, and have provisions that "keep the money together"—*and* the family together, too.

Without a trust or even with a boilerplate trust, you can count on the default outcome of "divide, distribute, and destroy," just as in the Vanderbilt family. If your assets go through probate, the court will make the choice, not you. And it will be public knowledge; all that you have or do not have will be on display. With a trust, you can "own nothing, control everything," a core mantra of the Rockefeller family.

You can make it so your heirs don't have to start over at zero with every generation, but instead can leverage your legacy to support their passion and purpose and live lives they love.

For example, if your descendants have a business idea, you may want to empower them to start that business with the family trust rather than leaving them to try and make it happen while working jobs. You may want to help your kids pay for their education so they aren't shackled with debt. You may want to empower them to make a bigger impact in the lives of others by encouraging them to make choices aligned with their purpose and with value creation in mind.

I want my trust to be a magnifying glass for good. If my heirs are not doing healthy, productive things, they won't get access to the trust. But if they are producing value, they will be empowered. For example, I have a deal with my kids if they read and write book reports. At one time (when they were likely too young), I told them I'd pay them $10,000 to read and write a report on *Atlas Shrugged*, yet updated the amount and book list over time. I also have other deals in place to encourage them to find and live their Soul Purpose. I've even created a worksheet you can use to personalize the teachings in your trust and Family Constitution. You'll find the worksheet in the Legacy Builder course, which you can get for free at rockefellersbook.com/legacy.

So instead of dropping money into their laps that could spoil them, leading to a life of unhappiness, my objective is to support my heirs in finding their purpose, creating a vision, and being value creators. I want to avoid creating "trust fund babies," and instead help to create producers in society. They will not be able to live lives of entitlement, but if they are good stewards, they will live privileged lives.

In the Rockefeller Method, you use a trust to protect and perpetuate your wealth and utilize optimally funded whole life insurance to fund the trust from generation to generation. It is a way to store your money without having to worry about market loss. It is a banking alternative that gives you stability, security, and liquidity. The financial structure is supported by a legacy structure of values and vision.

The financial strategy and the centerpiece that protects your economic value, today and in the future, is a properly structured, optimally funded whole life insurance policy with a participating mutual company. Whole Life Certified experts know the core of this methodology and have used it to power the Rockefeller Method.

Properly structured, optimally funded whole life insurance is the strategy for maximizing the tool of life insurance. It doesn't work because of the product: It works because of the strategy of looking cohesively and comprehensively at how things work together. Your overall financial blueprint is *the* key to guiding your financial choices.

Insurance is only one piece of the puzzle, albeit an important one. But what does legacy mean to you? Legacy is the total impact of the thoughts, ideas, values, signposts, examples, and influence we leave to those we love. Legacy includes not just the money we leave, but, more importantly, the lessons and instructions that come with that money. Legacy is our values, our actions, and our love passed down through generations.

No matter your profession or the current state of your finances, you can create a legacy. That is why I wrote this book. Because you are valuable. You and your family are worth it. You are not your bank account. You are not your circumstances or your mistakes. *You are lovable. You are loved.*

My parents gave me everything they could by instilling great values in me—a strong work ethic, resilience, and, most of all, love. Maybe you didn't receive the unconditional love, encouragement, and unwavering support my parents gave me. But you hold the pen. What will you write in the next chapter of your life? Will you overcome your doubts? Will you take responsibility for your next actions? Will you speak wealth into existence and expand it through new awareness and action?

It's your turn.

It is no accident that you are reading this.

It's your time.

CHAPTER 4

The Heart of the Rockefeller Method

I f you look at the Forbes list of the wealthiest families in the country today, you'll notice that the Rockefellers are still on that list. The Vanderbilts, on the other hand, are not. Why? Because the Rockefellers had a method for perpetuating and preserving wealth, rather than having each generation start over again. The Rockefellers kept their wealth centralized, which allowed their family to become stronger. Since they have a family trust, they don't have to beg banks for money. They can loan money to heirs, earning interest for their trust rather than paying it to financial institutions.

When most people die, their money just gets distributed and spent. Therefore, their wealth, and legacy, get destroyed. But with the Rockefeller Method, you can preserve your legacy and live prosperously along the way.

The Rockefeller Method is not about controlling everything from the grave. Rather, it is about giving successive generations parameters whereby they can tap into a family trust that operates as an alternative to banks. Even better, they have access to a board that holds some of the knowledge you would have bestowed on that generation, were you still alive.

You can set up a trust that allows your heirs to invest in education and expand their ability to earn a living and create value. This can mean paying for college, an entrepreneurial program, a mastermind program, etc. To access money, they could write a plan to the board of the trust, stating, "I'd like to go to this program, it costs this much money, and I'd like to borrow that money from the trust." The trust is essentially a bank replacement, utilizing a Family Office concept.

However, establishing a trust is not enough. Your trust must be funded with a properly structured, optimally funded whole life insurance policy that protects and replenishes the cash in the trust. This is the heart and the financial lifeblood of the Rockefeller Method.

HOW WHOLE LIFE INSURANCE FUELS THE ROCKEFELLER METHOD

With the Rockefeller Method, as soon as a beneficiary of your trust is born, the trust takes out a whole life policy for them and for the maximum amount of insurance the company will offer. That way, if an heir borrows money from the trust but isn't able to pay it back, it's not detrimental to the survival of the trust. Reason being, if that heir dies before paying back the loan, the life insurance death benefit replaces the money. It is also important to have a death benefit to replenish funds in case tax fluctuations, inflation, or economic turmoil create losses within the trust.

There can be safeguards, such as restrictions on how much an heir can borrow and ensuring that if they are unable to pay it back in full, the trust will be made whole again by the life insurance. And when an heir does pay back a loan, the interest is NOT paid to the government or a banking institution, but back into the family trust, keeping the family strong.

You can set up a trust like this for experiences, entrepreneurship, and any number of enterprises. You can structure it so that people can only borrow a certain amount or even a specific number of times, depending on the assets in the trust. The board you set up can use a Family Constitution. This is an extended family mission statement that will help govern their decisions and make sure the money is put to good use. (I have a thirty-eight-page Family Constitution for my board, and I'll share parts of it later in the book.) The board is a group of people you select that will best represent you in case of death. The board can help educate, mentor, and support the family while also protecting your wealth. We discuss how to establish your board in Chapter 12.

The Family Constitution allows for more dynamic management in an ever-changing, unpredictable future. It is governed by principles, values, and frameworks to inform decisions that will impact heirs. It gives enough structure, but not so much detail that it may be rendered irrelevant by technological advances and change.

Beware of Alternatives!

Some salespeople will offer alternatives with unlikely outcomes that put your capital, and therefore your legacy, at risk. The most common is indexed universal life (IUL), which creates unnecessary risk and can be a problem.

Some books and salespeople use marketing terms like "LASER fund" or "LIRP." These are sold as whole life alternatives, dependent on performance in the market, where funds buy options for the index to perform. But there is a cap rate (the upside is limited), and a myriad of other factors that are about chasing returns rather than protecting your money.

Don't be fooled. This is not the Rockefeller Method. Most people are using this as a tax-efficient alternative to investing, which means that there are additional risks, such as the cost of insurance potentially increasing and putting your capital at risk. If the increased cost isn't covered, the policy can lapse and even cause a taxable event.

What is Your "Investor DNA"?

Understanding the concept of Investor DNA is knowing who you are as a person first, then using that knowledge as a basis for determining which investments are a good fit for you, your family, and your business.

The core components of Investor DNA include:

1. **Core Values** are the ideals, ethics, and beliefs you deem important and esteem highly. They create a foundation for decision-making.

2. **Core Competencies** are your strengths, experiences, and the areas of life where you can create high levels of value.

3. **Core Drivers** are the priorities that motivate and energize you. They are essentially the "gas in the tank" that helps fuel you each day.

4. **Core Focus** is about the areas of life you're committed to, the places where you create rhythms and habits to bring forth results. We're taught to diversify investments, but diversification is the opposite of focus and will pull you away from what's most important to you. Often people de-worse-ify by spreading themselves thin and allocating money to things they do not understand.

The best investments for you are those that align with all four components of your Investor DNA Core Competencies, which are your strengths, experiences, and the areas of life where you can create high levels of value.

A MUCH BETTER ALTERNATIVE THAN BANKS

When it comes to saving, protecting, and growing your money, traditional banking is not your friend. First of all, the interest rate on savings was anemic for years. Recently, the Federal Reserve has been regularly raising rates and putting bond values at risk. Your bank account requires you to pay tax on interest earned. Cash in savings, money markets, and certificates of deposit are exposed to, not protected from, liability.

The FDIC has been inadequate at protecting the shortfalls in the past. There is now only $250,000 of protection on savings accounts, rather than the $300,000 from guarantee life associations on your life insurance cash value.

There has been a lot of volatility with banks in 2008 and 2009, as well as 2023. In 2008 and 2009, the FDIC was exposed because it was grossly underfunded and underinsured, requiring the government to infuse trillions of dollars into it due to a systemwide failure. Part of this problem comes from fractionalized banking. The bank lends out a dollar more than once, which is part of the reason for inflation and the exacerbated problem of default. 2023 was the biggest year ever for bank failures, and the Deposit Insurance Fund lost $16.3 billion.

Even if you don't currently have a banking alternative or trust to tap into, there are ways to pay interest back to your trust or the insurance company, allowing you to free up cash instead of paying mountains of interest to banks on mortgage loans, credit cards, or student loans.

Wouldn't you rather have a system that safeguards your wealth, grows your money, and provides stability and predictability while allowing you access to your money along the way?

You can—with properly structured, optimally funded whole life insurance.

Simply put, whole life insurance is a permanent policy where you can

It is important
to emphasize
that properly
structured,
optimally funded
life insurance is not
an investment.

use the cash value as a savings vehicle and bank alternative that has guarantees plus dividends. It can create a structure to save on insurance costs from term life, long-term care, or even taxes. You can save money in a properly structured, optimally funded whole life insurance program and coordinate those savings with all of your money-making decisions. You can use your own money instead of a bank's money and set up a loan scenario where you are in control of your payback periods and use your cash value to access money from the insurance company.

This can be an asset allocation choice instead of other fixed-income vehicles like bonds, money markets, or certificates of deposit. It removes the risk of capital depreciation when interest rates fluctuate because your cash values and minimum interest rates are guaranteed. This gives you access to money during times of distress or economic downturns. Not only does your money have minimum guarantees, but once a dividend is paid, it becomes guaranteed.

It is important to emphasize that properly structured, optimally funded life insurance is not an investment.

From a cash standpoint, it is a mid-term strategy to store your money with long-term legacy benefits. It gives you access to a myriad of benefits that allow for the Rockefeller Method. This includes a death benefit that grows with paid up additions and dividends.

However, there is a capitalization period. This means that for the first few years, you will have less cash value than you would with a savings account. If you set it up with the wrong company, don't fund it properly, or design it poorly, it could take a decade or longer to break even.

Optimally funded whole life allows you to retain control of your money rather than hand it over to a bank. Banks may or may not lend you money and you may or may not like their terms. With insurance, you can access your money anytime through a withdrawal or take out a loan from the insurance company. This allows you to keep your money earning interest while you borrow. It also gives you tax advantages.

Cash value is not likely to provide your highest rate of return. Your best return will come from something you access your cash value to invest in—something that aligns with your Investor DNA.

With an ideal financial plan, you can:

1. Minimize risk and prevent loss of money.

2. Minimize taxation on the money you accumulate.

3. Minimize taxation on the money you distribute.

4. Earn a rate of return on your money.

5. Have money available for use throughout your life.

6. Have contingencies for death, disability, emergencies, and unforeseen factors.

7. Have a systematic flow of money into your plan.

8. Have the flexibility to make changes to your plan.

9. Experience economic certainty.

You can do all of this with a strategy that integrates properly structured, optimally funded whole life.

When you have good credit, good collateral, and good cash flow, it's easy to get bank loans. But if one of those things is disrupted when it's time to get a loan, you are in trouble. When you utilize optimally funded whole life, you no longer have to apply for loans. You no longer have to use your credit to take out a loan. You don't have to fill out a bunch of paperwork. You don't have to deal with the slew of obstacles because you now have a system to access money inside your policy. It is your money, and you can do what you want with it.

Moreover, you have a flexible payback period. You get to choose how much and when you will pay back the loan. If the loan is utilized for business purposes, you may even be able to write off the interest! Instead of paying interest to the bank, you can earn interest on your money while borrowing from the insurance company—while building your legacy plan and Rockefeller-style trust at the same time.

Barring extraordinary circumstances or emergencies, it doesn't make sense to take out loans to pay for groceries or utilities. This money is there when opportunities arise or in times of downturn. When others are losing money, your money is secure and can be used to acquire assets during times of distress.

Don't keep the majority of your cash in banks where it's exposed, taxable, and without additional benefits. Instead, store your money where you gain additional advantages, including a death benefit, asset protection, and dividends.

Whole life insurance products offer guarantees from 2–4%, plus a probable dividend minus the cost of insurance. I'd only recommend companies that have paid above the guarantee for at least 100 years or more without missing a single dividend.

Depending on your age, your health, and how you fund these products, you can net between 1–6% (or higher, if interest rates keep increasing).

With a whole life policy, dividends typically move slower when interest rates increase or decrease.

SAVINGS ACCOUNT	OPTIMALLY FUNDED WHOLE LIFE
Taxable	Not as taxable as it grows (FIFO plus loan)
Interest	Minimum guaranteed interest plus dividend
No provision for disability	Waiver of premium
Must pay for LTC insurance	Accelerated benefit rider
Must pay for term insurance	Permanent death benefit
Not protected from liability and bankruptcy	Protected from liability and bankruptcy
Fully flexible	Very flexible
Fully liquid	Very liquid
Fairly safe financial institutions	Very safe financial institutions

COMPARING BANKS WITH INSURANCE CONTRACTS

Let's compare banks to insurance contracts. Insurance is FIFO—first in, first out. That means that if you take a withdrawal of your cash instead of a loan, you get the nontaxable money back first and gains second. The waiver of premium is a paid-for rider you can add (for an additional charge) that continues the funding of your policy if you are disabled for six months or longer. The accelerated benefit rider can be added at no charge and allows you to access your death benefit for items like long-term care. The cash 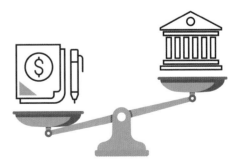 value is fully protected from liability and bankruptcy in 80% of states and partially protected in the rest.

Yet banks have their place. It makes sense to have some money in bank accounts to pay bills, for example. Banks have more flexibility because there is a period where funding is required for your insurance. In the early years of a whole life policy, you will have less cash value due to marketing expenses, underwriting costs, and the insurance company allocating funds for reserves.

In most cases, money stored in banks can be slightly more liquid. Getting an insurance loan typically takes around seventy-two hours, and in some cases a bit longer; whereas, hypothetically, you can wire money from your bank account on the same day. (I say "hypothetically" because I took my son to the bank to show him how wiring funds worked with the purchase of my home. After waiting forty-three minutes, we left the bank without success. The verification process required for that amount of money took days, not minutes.)

If you want to borrow money from your insurance, your cash value is your collateral and the insurance company issues the loan. You make a phone call or send in a form. They can send the money overnight (after twenty-four to forty-eight hours of processing time) or wire it to your account. You choose how you want to pay it back. You can treat it just like any other automatically paid loan, choosing when you want to pay extra and when you don't. You never have to disclose that you took out this kind of loan, so it won't affect your credit. The only requirement for getting the loan is that you have some cash in your policy to borrow.

When you put money in a bank, the bank puts a certain percentage of that money into life insurance as part of their reserve account. They do this because life insurance cash values have tax benefits and the dividends have outperformed other cash equivalents.[1]

Insurance companies have strict parameters for where they can invest

---

1   For more on this, check out https://bolicoli.com/boli

the money in their general portfolios. Since they aren't allowed to invest in anything too volatile, they make more stable investments.

Properly structured, optimally funded whole life insurance is instrumental in having cash when opportunities arise. It allows you to pay for your kid's college tuition, pay off inefficient loans, possibly finance your home or car, start a business, or have a peace of mind fund—and earn interest the whole time.

As Michael puts it, it increases your clarity and peace of mind by allowing you to *know* rather than *hope*. When you know that your savings are stored securely and where they will earn a guaranteed rate of interest, you can make financial decisions, run your business, and plan your life differently than you would when just hoping. Then you can leverage that certainty for planning in all other areas of your life. This is what the wealthy do.

Guard against uncertainty and stop feeling stressed about finances. Choose to take the money you're currently allocating to savings and redirect those dollars into your optimally funded whole life system. This will allow you to have liquidity, savings, a death benefit, and guarantees, and enable you to utilize your money along the way and for future financial decisions, all while benefiting you.

Mutual life insurance companies have proven to be one of the safest places to store cash. To see more on this, check out the annual reports and an article at wholelifecertified.com.

Put yourself in a financial position where you are free to choose the path you enjoy most. Ensure that your great-great-great-grandkids know not only your name but what your family stands for and how they can live their best lives. Find your path to financial independence, perpetuate your wealth, preserve your values, protect your family, and change their destiny—all through the Rockefeller Method.

CHAPTER 5

Leverage Living Benefits to Maximize Insurance

Term life offers only a death benefit in the event of your death. In contrast, permanent insurance offers not only a death benefit but also a variety of what we call "living benefits." These are—obviously—benefits you can take advantage of while you're alive.

Before I knew about the Rockefeller Method, I bought an insurance policy and set up a similar system without fully knowing what it was. I was looking to buy a new car and noticed that the previous year's models still on the lot were selling at lower prices, with great incentives. I found a deal that allowed me to save $262 per month by leasing for sixty months rather than buying the car. I chose the lease and put that extra $262 a month into an optimally funded whole life insurance policy.

With the extra money plus what I was saving on taxes by leasing, I was able to borrow cash from the insurance company based on the cash value of the policy and pay off the residual value of the car after thirty-nine months to become the owner. Then I took the money I would have spent on car payments and made a payment into the policy every month until the policy loan was paid off. The money was back in my policy—with interest.

From that day forward, I self-financed every car I bought and captured wealth in my optimally funded whole life policy rather than giving that money to a bank. It didn't matter what my credit score was—it was a completely private loan. And I had money growing on a tax-favored basis!

That was the beginning. When I started an internship with Guardian Life, I began to learn a little bit more about the living benefits of optimally funded whole life insurance plans. As I looked into other uses of life insurance beyond financing car purchases, I started to develop this process to create economic independence: Create enough cash flow from assets to cover expenses through plugging financial leaks, optimally fund a whole life insurance contract, and utilize the cash value when the right opportunities arise.

There are plenty of ways to increase cash flow now and in the future. There are so many methods and strategies for finding money and using whole life to create safety and liquidity; save tax; and protect cash from economic downturns, financial predators, and bankruptcy. I'll discuss these methods in detail later in the book.

As you read further, you will also discover how whole life can provide tax-free exit strategies for businesses or other assets subject to capital gain taxes. There are even ways to increase the cash flow from your other assets by coordinating assets with your death benefit. The right companies have new provisions that can eliminate the need for long-term care insurance. You can focus on building and creating cash flow rather than accumulating for thirty years into the future (or until age sixty-five, as retirement planning teaches us to do).

VALUE AND CAPITAL CAPTURE

Optimally funded whole life insurance has three key benefits:

1. It safeguards your wealth.
2. It helps you grow your money and increase your cash flow.
3. It helps you enjoy your money today *and* tomorrow.

In finance, we're usually taught that accumulating money for the long haul is the only way to grow wealth. However, the value and capital capture process with optimally funded whole life allows you to both prepare for the future *and* live wealthier today.

The value and capital capture process happens through the Rockefeller Method. The insurance policy supports the recovery of term insurance premiums, tax savings, and opportunity costs. It also protects against liability and premature death and can support increased cash flow by coordinating your death benefit to unlock assets.

Neither savings accounts, mutual funds, nor almost any other investment will fully protect your value today or preserve your capital with each gain. The next economic downturn doesn't have to reduce your capital, though. As you recover costs, you can capture the money in your cash value. When opportunities arise, you can use the cash value to capitalize quickly and invest.

As I mentioned previously, in the first few years of a whole life policy, you will be at a disadvantage from a cash standpoint. This happens because of the expenses involved with securing a large death benefit. The insurance company requires a certain reserve for the benefits and has several expenses in setting up the policy, including underwriting (testing blood and urine is part of this) and marketing costs (agent commissions, for example).

This doesn't mean you are in it for the long haul. It means that to secure these benefits, you will initially have a lower cash value before you break even and eventually end up with more cash in your policy than you would in a money market or certificate of deposit, or have similar returns to a bond portfolio with the same allocation.

How long it will take to surpass other savings vehicles with your cash value will depend on many factors, including:

1. Interest rates.

2. Policy design.

3. Paid-up additions (PUA), aka *funding optimally*.

4. Health ratings.

5. Enhanced dividends (for larger policies).

Again, this policy is not a replacement for investing, but rather a value and capital capture process to store your money until it is time to invest. It is a place to protect your economic replacement value, with the following benefits:

- When you die, your trust is funded, income tax-free.

- If you become disabled, the premiums are covered (assuming you have a waiver of premium rider).

- If you are sued, your money is either partially or fully protected (depending on the state in which you sign your policy).

- If the market goes down, your money is safe.

- You create contingencies for future cash flow by having a permanent death benefit (more explanation to come).

Use this method to automatically save and deliberately invest. The money will be available when opportunities arise.

CASH VALUE IS YOUR OPPORTUNITY FUND AND WAR CHEST

Optimally funded whole life insurance is a superior way to create your peace of mind fund, your opportunity fund, and a war chest.

An opportunity fund is money you set aside to utilize when you want to seize an investment at a moment's notice.

A war chest is money that you can use for any surprise that money can help you solve. Whether it's a lawsuit, a cash flow crunch, or the need to pay off a debt with a higher interest rate, the war chest is required to address what I call the "success tax." The more success you have, the greater the chance that people will come after what you have.

I've used my whole life insurance policy to seize opportunities for decades. I've bought a business, built a production studio, bought two cabins and several investment properties, and made a down payment on my current home by utilizing loans against my cash value.

A bank may have approved the loans for these types of requests, depending on several conditions. But even if they had, the process would have been much more difficult and time-consuming. The bank wants to see your taxes and credit score, have you pay for an appraisal, take hair, blood, and saliva samples, and get you to sign over your firstborn. Okay, maybe not those last two, but you get the point.

If I had needed money in 2008, banks would have denied any of my requests. This is because I already had too many properties financed. Relying on banks can be problematic if timing is an issue. With one of my cabins, time was of the essence, and I had the money from my policies within ten days. Two other people had made offers on that cabin, and the ability to move quickly was my key advantage.

Through cash value loans, I closed on the second cabin I purchased within five days (and had money in my account within seventy-two hours of my request).

When I published my *New York Times* bestselling book, *Killing Sacred Cows*, I jumped on the chance to save 66% off the normal rate for full-page ads in the *Wall Street Journal* and *New York Times* by requesting a loan against the cash value in my insurance. You can use your cash value insurance loans toward anything you want.

In 2008, I even used a loan against my cash value to pay off an American Express credit card balance with a 17% interest rate. The loan from the insurance company was 5%, which saved me the additional 12% that was going to AMEX. I paid back the loan on my terms, recapturing the 12% by adding more cash to one of my policies. Now I was earning—or, more accurately, saving—the interest rather than paying it. I captured that money in my policy instead of losing it.

Michael and I are not alone in leveraging the living benefits of whole life insurance. Here are several examples of famous people and businesses who have done the same.

FOSTER FARMS
1939

Max and Verda Foster borrowed $1,000 against their life insurance policy to invest in an eighty-acre chicken farm. Today, Foster Farms' products are sold all over the world.

DISNEYLAND
1953

To start his theme park, Disneyland, Walt Disney was unable to secure a large enough bank loan. So he borrowed against the cash value from his life insurance policy to fund it. Today, The Walt Disney Company has annual revenues of nearly $90 billion.

MCDONALD'S
1961

When Ray Kroc bought out the McDonald brothers, he used cash value from his two life insurance policies to cover the salaries of key employees. He also used the funds to pay for the marketing campaign for his new mascot, Ronald McDonald. The franchise has since grown to over 40,000 stores in 118 countries and counting.

PAMPERED CHEF
1980

Doris Christopher used a policy loan of $3,000 to start her new kitchenware company. The company was later purchased by Warren Buffet's Berkshire Hathaway for $1.5 billion.

SENATOR JOHN MCCAIN
2000

Senator McCain secured initial campaign financing for his presidential bid by using his life insurance policy as collateral.

UNINTERRUPTED COMPOUNDING

Some well-known financial gurus and authors say that to avoid unnecessary interest payments, you should never finance a car. In some cases, they're right. But if you use your optimally funded whole life, financing big purchases can actually make sense. The fact is, while financing costs you in interest payments, paying in full with cash costs you an opportunity.

This is called opportunity cost. Simply put, opportunity cost is what you miss out on when you choose one option over another. In other words, every decision you make in life includes an opportunity cost—the option you did not take. Opportunity costs can add up to thousands of dollars each year if you don't understand or acknowledge them.

However, taking out loans against the cash value from your insurance policy can make opportunity cost work in your favor. It can create positive cash flow that increases your wealth, all while allowing you to make those big purchases. How? Through the law of uninterrupted compounding.

Compounding is a strategy in which you earn interest, then take the interest you've earned at the end of that year and reinvest it with your original stake so it continues to earn a return (along with your principal). As this process repeats year after year, your earnings snowball and your wealth grows.

The longer you allow your money to compound uninterrupted, the more it grows. If you allow it to compound uninterrupted over many years—the key to successful compounding—it can produce a fortune.

For example, if you have $10,000 in an investment growing at 10% interest, over the first forty years, it'll grow to $452,593. That would be an unprecedented return because to get 10% a year without losses is unreasonable and unlikely in some years. I'm just giving you an illustration here. But with compounding and putting the interest back into the investment, something amazing happens. By year fifty, you'll have $1 million. By year sixty, you'll have more than $3 million. You might be too old to enjoy it, but you'll have it, right?

Here's the catch: This amazing growth can happen only if the compounding process is uninterrupted; in other words, if you never pull any money out of the account. For example, if you made an early withdrawal of $150,000 from your account in year forty, then in year fifty, you'd only have $745,000 instead of $1 million. By year sixty, you'd have $2 million instead of $3 million—a full $1 million less because of a $150,000 withdrawal. Even that small amount could cause your wealth to plummet.

The point is that interrupting the compounding process by liquidating all or even part of your funds is a destroyer of wealth. Unfortunately, these interruptions happen all the time without you even realizing it. Of course, if you have a 401(k), a decline of 20% in the stock market would interrupt the compounding process because your account balance would also drop by 20%.

When you pull money out of a bank account, brokerage account, or 401(k) for a big expense, you usually liquidate your savings account, sell your stock, or get rid of your mutual fund. This frees up your money for use on purchases but means that the money is no longer earning for you or participating in the compounding process.

As we've seen, this impacts your long-term returns. When you pay cash for big purchases, the compounding process is interrupted. However, when you pay for these same purchases using your insurance policy, the compounding process is not interrupted.

Why? Because when you take out a loan from your insurance, you're not taking money out of the policy, you're borrowing against it. The insurance company with whom you hold your life insurance policy will lend you money up to the amount you've saved in your policy, knowing that even if you don't pay it back, they can just deduct it from your death benefit when you die.

Because you're borrowing against your policy and not from it, the actual cash in your policy remains untouched. No money is removed from your account. Therefore, the money in your account can continue to compound and grow completely uninterrupted. Your cash value grows even when you have borrowed against it. Even when you are paying the loan back, your cash value is uninterrupted and compounding.

ALTERNATIVES TO WHOLE LIFE INSURANCE

Whole life is not the only vehicle you can use to save money and borrow from. But no savings vehicle has the same benefits as permanent life insurance.

Municipal bonds can work. However, in some cases, municipalities have defaulted on bonds—something that, decades ago, was unheard of and almost unprecedented in this country's history. In 1994, Orange County, California had a derivatives crisis and was going to default on its bonds, which changed bond rates for the whole state of California. In 2013, the city of Detroit declared bankruptcy and defaulted on bond payments as well. What was once considered a very safe investment doesn't seem as safe anymore.

In fact, what's riskiest about municipal bonds is that the value of existing bonds can go down, as they did with rising interest rates in 2022 and 2023. That's called capital depreciation, meaning you could lose the principal value of your bond.

If, on the other hand, your money is in an insurance policy, you have no capital deprecation risk once dividends are declared. As the foundation of your Rockefeller Method system, optimally funded whole life stacks up extremely well when compared with other savings vehicles, including savings accounts, certificates of deposit, checking accounts, and money market accounts.

Those accounts performed at a lower rate than the declared dividend for decades. But with the hike in interest rates in 2022 and 2023, dividends on insurance are now lagging. That is the nature of interest and dividends for cash value—slower to rise and slower to lower.

With optimally funded whole life, you have a guaranteed interest rate plus a non-guaranteed dividend that can push up your returns. You can access your money without penalties and with tax advantages so you can pursue that deal of a lifetime when it comes along. You have access to your money for whatever reason you need it, whether that is buying a home or a business or paying off a credit card.

Retirement plans could work because you can borrow from them. But there is no guarantee of principal without moving to a money market at a low interest rate. Nor is there a death benefit. There are strict limits on how much you can borrow and no flexibility in the repayment schedule. Plus, you cannot fund extra on the loan amount and thereby capture a potential interest spread for yourself; you pay back the amount of the loan and nothing more. With paid-up additions (PUA) and cash value, however, you can take the difference between the interest you would pay a bank and what you pay for the life insurance loan and add it to your cash value.

Certificates of deposit and certain types of bonds are fairly safe, but you may incur penalties if you liquidate them. In some cases, you can get a line of credit or loan against a certificate of deposit. However, this lacks key advantages since a certificate of deposit is taxable and typically gives you a lower interest rate than you can get with whole life dividends.

I also don't like leaving money in a certificate of deposit or money market account because it is subject to creditors, and simply because banks are riskier.

Whole life offers a consistent, guaranteed return, along with powerful tax advantages and significant liquidity. If interest rates go up or down, your principal is safe with whole life because when you have your cash value and your dividends have been paid, you are guaranteed a minimum interest rate. That means you won't have capital depreciation. You'll have stability and predictability. For business owners, stability and predictability are of significant value.

I constantly look for business and investment opportunities. Having cash value in my whole life policies allows me to take advantage of those opportunities. Using whole life cash value loans, I've bought into businesses, paid off real estate and credit cards, and purchased a production studio and video equipment. I've also found a way to recapture all the insurance costs through an allocation of my money to this system. Because of my cash value and death benefit, I'm able to eliminate term insurance, raise deductibles on my car and home insurance, and extend elimination periods on disability insurance.

It is also important to note that if an insurance company goes out of business, your money is much more likely to remain secure than it would be with a different type of institution.

When Executive Life went out of business in the 1980s, no policyholder lost money because another company acquired all the accounts without having to pay a commission to build that book of business. Even if an insurance company goes out of business and another company doesn't buy it out, every state in the US has guarantees on death benefits and the cash value in policies.

Overall, insurance companies are much more stable and predictable than pretty much any other financial institution. As we mentioned earlier, an optimally funded whole life insurance policy is set up for the whole of your life. If you live to 120, this policy still works!

THE HISTORY AND USE OF LIFE INSURANCE

Life insurance is one of the oldest financial products in existence, with sales beginning in the US in the late 1760s. It has survived a revolution, a civil war, two world wars, and multiple depressions and recessions. During the Great Depression, over 9,000 banks went bankrupt. In contrast, only 2% of the total assets of all life insurance companies in the United States were impaired between 1929 and 1938.

In fact, the strength of the insurance industry is a big part of what helped when the same thing happened during the 2008 financial crisis. Of the safest insurance companies, only 1% had "non-performing" investments. The financial crisis did not affect these companies, and they were able to continue paying dividends.

Life insurance policies were once prevalent. After World War I, there were nearly 120 million life insurance policies in effect in the United States. That's about one for every US citizen at the time! People had these policies not just for the death benefit, but also for the cash value. They were so common that they even showed up in the movies. In *It's a Wonderful Life*, Jimmy Stewart's character bargains with his adversary using the cash value of his whole life insurance policy!

Life insurance is at the heart of building financial security and independence today and for the future. But most people don't understand it and therefore don't consider it essential at all! The number of people who have life insurance has fallen from 72% in the 1960s to just 44% in 2010. People tend to fall into four categories when it comes to insurance: they hate it and avoid buying it whenever possible; they hate it but begrudgingly buy the minimum amount; they like it but don't use it properly; or they understand it, love it, and use it to its full potential.

I like to get as much life insurance as an insurance company will offer on my life, and I like to put in as much extra cash as they'll allow. Once I do that, I insure my wife in the same way, then my kids, and even my business partners. Then, once the money moves above what I need for my peace of mind fund, I decide when I will use that cash.

For an entrepreneur, an optimally funded whole life policy is most effective when used as an opportunity fund or even a war chest. It provides liquidity when you want it, and when you access the money, you don't have to write a business plan or meet with a banker to explain the opportunity. All you have to do is fill out a form, and the money shows up in around seventy-two hours.

I've used cash from my whole life policy to pay off loans, finance businesses, do hard money loans, secure inventory at a discount, make down payments on real estate, and even buy out real estate partners. Then, once I've used the money on one of those opportunities, I restore that access to cash as quickly as possible.

Michael Explains How Clients Leverage Whole Life

One of the most common ways we and our clients leverage the living benefits of whole life insurance is to fund auto loans. In fact, as I write this, my son Kadin is doing it, as is my assistant, Lacey, and multiple clients.

Wendy and I started paying into an optimally funded whole life policy for Kadin when he was young. We've paid $350 per month into it for over twenty years now, and it currently has about $130,000 in cash value. When Kadin bought his new car, he took out a $20,000 loan from his policy. The life insurance company loaned him $20,000 at 5% interest and put a $20,000 lien against his cash value.

When looking to purchase a car, Kadin checked out interest rates with various banks and credit unions and was quoted 7.5–8% interest on auto loans. Instead of getting a loan through them, he took out a loan from his policy, using his cash value as collateral. His cash in the policy continues to grow uninterrupted. He used the current auto loan rate at the local bank, 7.5%, to pay himself back. 5% interest went back to the life insurance company, but he kept the 2.5% spread. His policy continues to grow uninterrupted while he borrows the money.

The spread between his cash value loan interest rate and the bank auto loan interest rate is only 2.5%. However, this represents a 50% better return, comparatively!

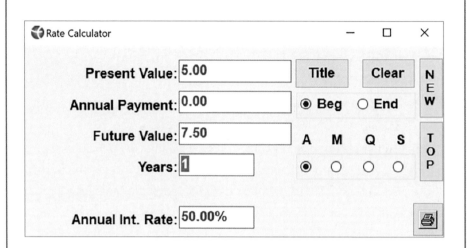

Present Value: 5.00   Title   Clear   N E W

Annual Payment: 0.00   ● Beg ○ End

Future Value: 7.50   A   M   Q   S   T O P

Years: 1   ● ○ ○ ○

Annual Int. Rate: 50.00%

This example could be used for any investment that yields a positive rate of return on a taxable basis. For example, one of my clients, Troy, does hard money loans. When I met Troy, he was taking cash from his regular bank account and lending it to others. For ease of calculation, I'm going to assume 10% earnings on his money. If Troy took $10,000 cash from his regular bank account, loaned it to someone, and made a 10% return, that would be a $1,000 gain in a year. If he were in a 30% total tax bracket, he would pay $300 in tax, netting him $700.

But what if Troy were to optimally fund a whole life policy and use the cash value, instead of his personal bank account, to lend to borrowers? Let's assume he does the same deal and borrows $10,000 against his cash value, lends it out, and makes a $1,000 profit in interest. However, before he pays taxes on the $1,000, he writes off the $500 he pays the life insurance company to borrow the $10,000 through the policy loan. This leaves him with a net taxable gain of $500.

In his case, it was 5% to borrow the $10,000 from his policy; 5% on $10,000 is $500 in interest paid to the life insurance company. A $1,000 gain minus the $500 paid to borrow the $10,000 is a net taxable

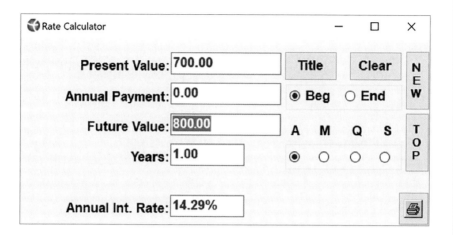

Rate Calculator — □ ✕

Present Value:	700.00
Annual Payment:	0.00
Future Value:	800.00
Years:	1.00
Annual Int. Rate:	14.29%

Title | Clear | N E W

◉ Beg ○ End

A M Q S | T O P

◉ ○ ○ ○

gain of $500. The 30% tax on the $500 gain is $150, and $150 minus the $500 equals a net $350.

But that's not the end of the story. Because he uses his cash value as collateral for the loan, the life insurance company puts a lien against the cash value. The cash value grows tax-free by 4.5%—for a total of $450.

A $350 net gain plus $450 is $800. This is opposed to the $700 net gain Troy would realize if he used a regular bank account for this type of investment. While $700 to $800 is a $100 gain, it also represents a 14.29% profit.

Other clients have used this strategy for equipment loans and leases, and to inject cash surpluses into their businesses.

To dive deeper into the numbers, visit rockefellersbook. com/auto. There, we compare three different ways to buy a car: on credit, with cash, and using cash value loans. We assume that you buy a new car every five years and do the math over a twenty-year period.

If your policy is designed well, optimally funded, and has built up enough cash value, you can take out a loan for 90% or more against the cash value within the first year. Notice that I said "against," not "from." When you take out a loan from your whole life insurance, you are not borrowing from your policy, but against it. Therefore, your policy continues to grow as if you hadn't taken out a loan at all; you do not actually take any cash out of the policy, but rather use its cash value as collateral.

Your cash value continues to grow with dividends.

Moreover, you never have to rush to repay the loan out of your cash flow. In fact, most insurance companies don't care if you miss a payment or several payments—or even if you pay them back at all. If you don't pay them back, all that happens is the balance is deducted when your death benefit is paid out.

Michael Does the Math

In one of the following illustrations, the client pays the interest on the policy loan each year; in the other, they do not. In both cases, the cash value and death benefit continue to grow.

Insured: Valued Client
Male, Age 40, Preferred Plus Non-Tobacco
Contract Premium Mode: Annual
EPPUA Premium Mode: Annual
Policy Payment Period: 60 Years
Initial Premium: $15,000.00

Initial Base Face Amount: $151,149
Initial Flexible Protection Rider Face Amount: $151,148
Initial Total Face Amount: $302,297
Initial Dividend Option: Paid-Up Additions (PUAs)

Supplemental Ledger - Current Dividend Scale

Values
Current Dividend Scale
Refer back to the basic illustration for guaranteed elements and other important information.

Values are based on the guarantees in your policy, as well as any non-guaranteed dividends paid at the current scale. This supplemental ledger will also reflect PUA/dividend surrenders and policy loans, if illustrated.

Benefits and values are subject to change by Penn Mutual and are not guaranteed, actual results may be more or less favorable.

Non-Guaranteed

Year	Age	Total Premium	Dividend	Premium Outlay	Cum. Premium Outlay	Income	Total Loan Balance	Total Net Cash Value	Change in Total Net Cash Value	Change in Net CV Less Prem. Outlay	Total Net Death Benefit w/out Div	Total Net Death Benefit
1	41	15,000	301	15,000	15,000	0	0	11,205	11,205	-3,795	334,776	335,077
2	42	15,000	634	15,000	30,000	0	0	23,654	12,449	-2,551	369,207	369,841
3	43	15,000	984	15,000	45,000	0	0	38,074	14,419	-581	403,756	404,741
4	44	15,000	1,427	15,000	60,000	0	0	53,954	15,880	880	438,448	439,875
5	45	15,000	2,130	15,000	75,000	0	0	71,315	17,361	2,361	473,296	475,426
6	46	15,000	2,603	15,000	90,000	0	0	89,235	17,921	2,921	508,333	510,936
7	47	15,000	3,134	15,000	105,000	0	0	108,187	18,952	3,952	543,576	546,710
8	48	15,000	3,661	15,000	120,000	0	0	128,192	20,004	5,004	579,051	582,713
9	49	15,000	4,214	15,000	135,000	0	0	149,306	21,115	6,115	614,779	618,993
10 [1]	50	15,000	4,658	16,079	151,079	20,000	20,000	151,448	2,142	-13,937	630,775	635,432
11 [1]	51	15,000	5,421	16,079	167,157	0	20,000	174,855	23,407	7,328	666,727	672,148
12 [1]	52	15,000	6,093	16,079	183,236	0	20,000	199,534	24,679	8,601	703,319	709,412
13 [1]	53	15,000	6,803	16,079	199,314	0	20,000	225,544	26,010	9,932	740,288	747,091
14 [1]	54	15,000	7,554	16,079	215,393	0	20,000	252,948	27,403	11,325	777,670	785,224
15 [1]	55	15,000	8,358	16,079	231,471	0	20,000	281,820	28,873	12,794	815,502	823,860
16 [1]	56	15,000	9,217	16,079	247,550	0	20,000	311,957	30,137	14,058	853,831	863,048
17 [1]	57	15,000	10,110	16,079	263,628	0	20,000	343,670	31,713	15,634	892,712	902,823
18 [1]	58	15,000	11,055	16,079	279,707	0	20,000	377,029	33,359	17,280	932,163	943,218
19 [1]	59	15,000	12,044	16,079	295,785	0	20,000	412,092	35,064	18,985	972,228	984,272
20 [1]	60	15,000	13,120	16,079	311,864	0	20,000	448,951	36,858	20,780	1,012,937	1,026,057
21 [1]	61	2,917	13,965	3,996	315,859	0	20,000	476,254	27,303	23,308	1,033,527	1,047,492
22 [1]	62	2,917	14,901	3,996	319,855	0	20,000	504,964	28,710	24,715	1,054,832	1,069,732
23 [1]	63	2,917	15,913	3,996	323,851	0	20,001	535,170	30,205	26,210	1,076,937	1,092,850
24 [1]	64	2,917	16,963	3,996	327,846	0	20,001	566,901	31,731	27,735	1,099,905	1,116,868
25 [1]	65	2,917	18,040	3,996	331,842	0	20,001	600,193	33,292	29,297	1,123,745	1,141,785

Insured: **Valued Client**

Male, Age 40, Preferred Plus Non-Tobacco
Contract Premium Mode: Annual
EPPUA Premium Mode: Annual
Policy Payment Period: 60 Years
Initial Premium: $15,000.00

Initial Base Face Amount: $151,149
Initial Flexible Protection Rider Face Amount: $151,148
Initial Total Face Amount: $302,297
Initial Dividend Option: Paid-Up Additions (PUAs)

Supplemental Ledger - Current Dividend Scale

Values

Current Dividend Scale
*Refer back to the basic illustration
for guaranteed elements and other
important information.*

*Benefits and values are subject to
change by Penn Mutual and are not
guaranteed, actual results may be
more or less favorable.*

Values are based on the guarantees in your policy, as well as any non-
guaranteed dividends paid at the current scale. This supplemental ledger will
also reflect PUA/dividend surrenders and policy loans, if illustrated.

Non-Guaranteed

Year	Age	Total Premium	Dividend	Premium Outlay	Cum. Premium Outlay	Income	Total Loan Balance	Total Net Cash Value	Change in Total Net Cash Value	Change in Net CV Less Prem. Outlay	Total Net Death Benefit w/out Div	Total Net Death Benefit
1	41	15,000	301	15,000	15,000	0	0	11,205	11,205	-3,795	334,776	335,077
2	42	15,000	634	15,000	30,000	0	0	23,654	12,449	-2,551	369,207	369,841
3	43	15,000	984	15,000	45,000	0	0	38,074	14,419	-581	403,756	404,741
4	44	15,000	1,427	15,000	60,000	0	0	53,954	15,880	880	438,448	439,875
5	45	15,000	2,130	15,000	75,000	0	0	71,315	17,361	2,361	473,296	475,426
6	46	15,000	2,603	15,000	90,000	0	0	89,235	17,921	2,921	508,333	510,936
7	47	15,000	3,134	15,000	105,000	0	0	108,187	18,952	3,952	543,576	546,710
8	48	15,000	3,661	15,000	120,000	0	0	128,192	20,004	5,004	579,051	582,713
9	49	15,000	4,214	15,000	135,000	0	0	149,306	21,115	6,115	614,779	618,993
10	50	15,000	4,650	15,000	150,000	20,000	21,140	150,301	994	-14,006	629,635	634,285
11	51	15,000	5,420	15,000	165,000	0	22,345	172,501	22,200	7,200	664,364	669,784
12	52	15,000	6,091	15,000	180,000	0	23,619	195,904	23,404	8,404	699,679	705,769
13	53	15,000	6,800	15,000	195,000	0	24,985	220,565	24,661	9,661	735,297	742,097
14	54	15,000	7,551	15,000	210,000	0	26,388	246,542	25,977	10,977	771,250	778,801
15	55	15,000	8,354	15,000	225,000	0	27,892	273,906	27,364	12,364	807,570	815,924
16	56	15,000	9,212	15,000	240,000	0	29,482	302,447	28,541	13,541	844,300	853,512
17	57	15,000	10,104	15,000	255,000	0	31,162	332,473	30,026	15,026	881,490	891,594
18	58	15,000	11,048	15,000	270,000	0	32,939	364,047	31,574	16,574	919,152	930,200
19	59	15,000	12,036	15,000	285,000	0	34,816	397,224	33,177	18,177	957,325	969,361
20	60	15,000	13,110	15,000	300,000	0	36,801	432,087	34,863	19,863	996,034	1,009,144
21	61	2,917	13,954	2,917	302,917	0	38,898	457,281	25,193	22,276	1,014,508	1,028,462
22	62	2,917	14,888	2,917	305,834	0	41,115	483,760	26,479	23,562	1,033,575	1,048,464
23	63	2,917	15,899	2,917	308,752	0	43,459	511,606	27,846	24,929	1,053,314	1,069,213
24	64	2,917	16,948	2,917	311,669	0	45,936	540,842	29,236	26,318	1,073,781	1,090,729
25	65	2,917	18,023	2,917	314,586	0	48,555	571,496	30,654	27,737	1,094,976	1,112,999

With that said, we will always encourage you to pay back the loan and allow that money (and more) to be used for future loans.

Borrowing against your whole life cash value policy will never affect your credit, since there is no such thing as a late payment. Additionally, if the loan is for your business, in most cases the interest you pay on it is tax-deductible.

Beware of Alternatives!

An important note: Some agents use other types of insurance to "arbitrage" borrowing. This means they have a variable loan that they hope will be less than the amount being earned in cash value. In some cases, the interest earned can be more than the interest paid. But it depends on economic factors like interest rate fluctuations and market performance. Often, they do not show what happens when the opposite occurs: The loan ends up costing more than the cash in the policy is being credited/earned. This adds instability and is at odds with the Rockefeller Method of mitigating risk to perpetuate wealth.

Do not jeopardize your cash value or chase returns that risk your capital. An insurance contract is meant to be predictable, available, and sustainable. This is not how you generate your greatest returns, but how you guarantee that money is accessible when the right opportunity comes along.

THE FOUNDATION OF YOUR FINANCIAL HOUSE

The living benefits of whole life insurance cannot be overstated. The cash value gives you quick access to loans without credit checks, provides tax-free money, and allows for capital preservation without risking principal. This cash value is considered a private account. If you have a child going to college, it won't affect your child's ability to get student loans. If the government changes the laws on retirement plans, it won't impact your money.

When structured properly, the death benefit enables you to pass more money to future generations without incurring estate taxes. In times of declining interest rates, insurance companies decrease the dividend rate more slowly, therefore offering higher rates than banks. Your cash and death benefit are fully protected from lawsuits and bankruptcy in over forty states and partially protected in all states.

The return from optimally funded whole life is comparable to a bond portfolio, with less risk. But it also has an excellent *external* rate of return. This term describes all the factors affected by a product, including what it allows you to accomplish, tax and insurance cost savings, mindset, quality of life, and additional benefits and byproducts the product creates. Byproducts like certainty, ability to access cash before 59.5, dividends, and guarantees.

Whole life is just the beginning, a part of the process. In reality, this is about putting your whole financial house in order.

CHAPTER 6

Turn Small Assets into Big Ones

Most retirees live in fear of economic change, as they are living off the interest from their nest eggs. Risk arises whenever the market shifts, taxes go up, interest rates change, or inflation diminishes purchasing power. Without the Rockefeller Method, the retirement dream feels more like a ream—the reaming out of waiting for years of your life, doing the things you hate to make and invest money, to finally afford the things you want. When you are too old to enjoy them? Do you think I want to go skiing when I am 85 and might break a hip? The only thing that happens when you are 85 is you wake up—and most days you don't want that to happen.

There is a much better way to retire: by utilizing your life insurance death benefit while you're alive. There's an old axiom that nobody ever gets wealthy from life insurance while they're alive. That may be true for most life insurance policies. But thanks to a major asset in your optimally funded whole life insurance policy, the permanent death benefit, that axiom doesn't have to be true for you.

Car insurance allows you to drive your car without fear of loss. Likewise, permanent life insurance allows you to live your life and spend your money without fear of either running out of money or failing to leave anything for your heirs. With whole life insurance, the death benefit is guaranteed to be in effect exactly one day longer than you. Therefore, you can leverage the certainty of your death to both spend more money while you're alive *and* preserve your family's long-term wealth and legacy.

This process of "turning small assets into big assets"[2] is about coordinating your death benefit to increase your cash flow. Your death benefit unlocks assets that would otherwise remain trapped.

The accumulation phase of your life is when you save and invest money during your working years. The distribution phase is when you start distributing your savings back to yourself in retirement. Your death benefit allows you to spend as much as 50% more cash flow when you get into the distribution phase of your life—with certainty.

HOW A DEATH BENEFIT REDUCES RISK AND INCREASES CASH FLOW

A death benefit enables you to coordinate and structure the distribution phase of your life with the greatest efficiency. Your death benefit benefits you while you're alive. This is possible because you know there will be a payout when you die. You can spend down your principal because whatever you spend while you're alive, your death benefit will replace for your heirs when you die. Therefore, you get to spend both the interest you accrue and the principal in the later years of your life. You get to spend more, pay less in taxes, hedge inflation, and limit your dependence on the stock market.

Even if the market went down 30% during your retirement, your lifestyle wouldn't have to be affected thanks to the death benefit and its impact on your future cash flow. Meanwhile, you can preserve your legacy for your family by using your insurance to replenish a trust completely tax-free.

---

2 "Turning small assets into big assets" is a term coined by a mentor of mine, Vince D'Addona. I use it with his permission.

The number one advantage of a death benefit is knowing for certain that there's a lump sum of money coming on the day you die. The date of your death is uncertain, but the fact that the sum of money will arrive on that date is not. And you can capitalize on that certainty to improve your cash flow while you're alive.

You can do this through the various means discussed in this chapter, and everywhere else in this book, including by utilizing a reverse mortgage, a charitable trust, or a paydown strategy. A death benefit will allow you, with planning, to simply accelerate the rate at which you spend money you have rather than leave it with the institutions.

The fear of running out of money controls the majority of people in their distribution phase. They might spend too aggressively. Economic turmoil or new advancements in longevity could occur. If any of these happen and you run out of money, you still have options. You can sell your death benefit. If you live to be 100 (or 120, depending on your policy), you can cash out your death benefit, allowing you to spend your death benefit while you're alive.

Here's an analogy: Imagine that you have an eccentric uncle who loves gold. One day, you get a call telling you that your uncle has died and left you $2 million in gold bars. However, there's a caveat: He has stipulated that you will not receive that gold until you turn eighty.

Can that $2 million in gold change your life today, even though you won't see it until you're eighty? Absolutely—now that you know for certain you'll receive the gold when you turn eighty. If you know the money will exist when you're eighty, you can spend money differently right now, before you turn eighty.

A death benefit is similar to a future inheritance. You can leverage the certainty of it coming in, even though you don't know exactly when that will happen.

OTHER SPECIFIC WAYS TO UTILIZE YOUR DEATH BENEFIT

There are other very specific ways to utilize your death benefit during your lifetime. Some of these benefits are already part of your policy. Riders are available on death benefits that ensure you for long-term care. If you can't perform two of what are known as the activities of daily living, this rider will allow you to spend up to 70% of your death benefit while you're alive.

Other ways to leverage your death benefit may sound a little morbid and are not necessarily what I'd recommend—viatical settlements, for example. A viatical settlement is when someone with a terminal illness sells his or her death benefit on the market. Not a particularly uplifting proposition.

A less morbid version of this is what is called a senior life settlement. Death benefits have such value that investors are willing to buy them for more than the cash value of the policy. Warren Buffett has bought billions of dollars in death benefits through senior life settlements. Buffett knows his company will be around longer than the policyholder. Through the law of large numbers, Buffet can assess what those guaranteed death benefit payouts will be worth to Berkshire Hathaway, his company.

In my opinion, neither viatical nor senior life settlements are the best way to draw a living benefit from your death benefit. In fact, the best living advantage of a death benefit is having a coordinated strategy to spend your assets, including your principal, because you have a guaranteed benefit that will go to your beneficiaries no matter what. Instead of just living off of interest, you can take full advantage of all your assets during the later years of your life, just as the Rockefeller family does and did.

A senior life settlement would merely be a backup strategy for a worst-case scenario in which you outlived your money. It would give you more peace of mind and more options in the future. This has some obvious advantages in terms of how much money you can spend every year, as we illustrate with our calculations in Appendix 1.

If you have a pension or annuity, there are several options for distribution. Option number one is the highest pension payout every single month for you, leaving nothing for a surviving spouse or kids when you die. The other options reduce the monthly payment more and more to leave money to your spouse or kids. However, if you have a death benefit, you don't have to worry about continuing your pension after you die. Your spouse and heirs will be provided for by your death benefit, and the money will be income tax-free.

Through pension maximization, you will ensure the highest cash flow without putting your heirs at risk. You do not have to guess or play the odds. The death benefit is guaranteed, whereas the lower monthly cash flow options create protection that is not guaranteed (if you die before your spouse, for example). Without a death benefit, you limit what you can take in cash flow. A certainty comes with your death benefit: When you die, your trust will be funded and your family will be taken care of. This allows you to increase your cash flow.

Paydown Strategy

Another benefit your life insurance can bring is the ability to take principal *and* interest. Instead of living off your interest alone, with every dollar subject to tax, you can spend down with an accelerated cash flow strategy. This can even protect you if taxes go up or in low-interest-rate environments.

The number one thing to protect against—and something that many people overlook—is inflation. If you're living off a fixed income in your later years, that income will lose purchasing power each year as the cost of living continues to rise. Inflation is like a stealth tax. With whole life insurance, you can offset the impact of inflation through your ability to spend your principal as well as your interest. Unless your money is in a tax-deferred qualified plan, the money you pull from your principal is tax-free.

By taking more than interest, you pay less in tax every year during the distribution phase. Your taxes drop year by year because even if tax rates rise, you take more and more principal, which has already been taxed, and earn less and less interest as you utilize your money.

Michael Does the Math

The following chart shows potential retirement income distributions based on two strategies.

In the first strategy, Distribution 1, the client "bought term and invested the difference" and has saved $2 million by retirement. Since the client dropped term insurance and is now "self-insured," they will only live off the interest of their $2 million. At an assumed annual interest rate of 5%, this means the client will withdraw $100,000 per year. Over twenty-five years and after taxes, the net distributions will be $2,162,581.

In the second strategy, Distribution 2, the client bought whole life insurance and accumulated $2 million in cash value by retirement age. But since the client isn't worried about running out of money and disinheriting heirs, they can withdraw much more money over time. Over a twenty-five period, this client can withdraw a total of $3,362,785 for retirement. (This is assuming that the twenty-five-year paydown starts at age sixty-five.)

Again, whole life gives you a permission slip to spend down your assets while you're alive! Without this permission slip, you are relegated to living solely off of interest for the rest of your life.

Distribution

Distribution 1

PV of Assets: 2,000,000
Earnings Rate: 5.00%
Withdrawal: 100,000.00 $ ○ Beg ◉ End
Steady Net Withdrawal Increase: %
Tax Method: On Earnings | Deductible | Deferred | Free
Int.Only | PayOn

YEAR	Beg. Of Year Acct. Value	Earnings Rate	Gross Withdrawal	Tax Payment	Net Spendable
7	2,000,000	5.00%	(100,000)	(13,497)	86,503
8	2,000,000	5.00%	(100,000)	(13,497)	86,503
9	2,000,000	5.00%	(100,000)	(13,497)	86,503
10	2,000,000	5.00%	(100,000)	(13,497)	86,503
11	2,000,000	5.00%	(100,000)	(13,497)	86,503
12	2,000,000	5.00%	(100,000)	(13,497)	86,503
13	2,000,000	5.00%	(100,000)	(13,497)	86,503
14	2,000,000	5.00%	(100,000)	(13,497)	86,503
15	2,000,000	5.00%	(100,000)	(13,497)	86,503
16	2,000,000	5.00%	(100,000)	(13,497)	86,503
17	2,000,000	5.00%	(100,000)	(13,497)	86,503
18	2,000,000	5.00%	(100,000)	(13,497)	86,503
19	2,000,000	5.00%	(100,000)	(13,497)	86,503
20	2,000,000	5.00%	(100,000)	(13,497)	86,503
21	2,000,000	5.00%	(100,000)	(13,497)	86,503
22	2,000,000	5.00%	(100,000)	(13,497)	86,503
23	2,000,000	5.00%	(100,000)	(13,497)	86,503
24	2,000,000	5.00%	(100,000)	(13,497)	86,503
25	2,000,000	5.00%	(100,000)	(13,497)	86,503
TOTAL	2,000,000	5.00%	2,500,000	(337,420)	2,162,581

Distribution 1 | Distribution 2 | Compare
Illustration Period (Years): 25   Inflation:
Federal Income Tax Table: 2021 ∨   Married ∨
State Income Tax Rate: ?Tax Credit For Losses ☑
Additional Income:
PLI Inputs | Include PLI?   Include Other Net Income?
Clear | New
Title

Distribution 2

PV of Assets: 2,000,000
Earnings Rate: 5.00%
Withdrawal: 141,904.91 $ ○ Beg ◉ End
Steady Net Withdrawal Increase: %
Tax Method: On Earnings | Deductible | Deferred | Free
Int.Only | PayOn

YEAR	Beg. Of Year Acct. Value	Earnings Rate	Gross Withdrawal	Tax Payment	Net Spendable
7	1,714,966	5.00%	(141,905)	(10,361)	131,544
8	1,658,810	5.00%	(141,905)	(9,744)	132,161
9	1,599,845	5.00%	(141,905)	(9,201)	132,704
10	1,537,933	5.00%	(141,905)	(8,829)	133,075
11	1,472,924	5.00%	(141,905)	(8,439)	133,465
12	1,404,666	5.00%	(141,905)	(8,030)	133,875
13	1,332,994	5.00%	(141,905)	(7,600)	134,305
14	1,257,739	5.00%	(141,905)	(7,148)	134,757
15	1,178,721	5.00%	(141,905)	(6,674)	135,231
16	1,095,752	5.00%	(141,905)	(6,176)	135,729
17	1,008,635	5.00%	(141,905)	(5,654)	136,251
18	917,162	5.00%	(141,905)	(5,105)	136,800
19	821,115	5.00%	(141,905)	(4,529)	137,376
20	720,266	5.00%	(141,905)	(3,923)	137,981
21	614,374	5.00%	(141,905)	(3,288)	138,617
22	503,188	5.00%	(141,905)	(2,621)	139,284
23	386,442	5.00%	(141,905)	(1,932)	139,973
24	263,859	5.00%	(141,905)	(1,319)	140,586
25	135,148	5.00%	(141,905)	(676)	141,229
TOTAL	0	5.00%	3,547,623	(184,838)	3,362,785

You may be wondering, *What happens if I spend down my principal and I'm still alive at ninety with nothing left in that account?* Your death benefit comes into play as a backstop. There are several ways you can tap into your life insurance death benefit and/or strategically coordinate the paydown of assets with other assets. The point is that the death benefit gives you permission to spend and enjoy more and still leave money behind. When you don't have a death benefit, your assets become your life insurance and the fear of scarcity is so great you won't end up spending the principal of your assets. It will then literally become the money you leave to your estate. Do it strategically and enjoy more *and* leave more.

Reverse Mortgages

If you have a home with equity, you can use your death benefit as collateral and secure a reverse mortgage. With a reverse mortgage, you can access tax-free money from the bank either in a lump sum or systematic payments. Rather than a mortgage, where you make payments to a bank, in a reverse mortgage, the bank makes payments to you. Since these payments are considered a loan, you don't have to pay tax on the money.

In a reverse mortgage, your home is normally the collateral. However, you can use your whole life death benefit instead so that when you die, the reverse mortgage is paid off with the death benefit rather than with your home. This turns an asset that isn't providing cash flow into a "bigger asset" by unlocking the equity in your home on a tax-free basis, providing a living benefit for you in your distribution phase.

This option may not even be the most efficient way to utilize your death benefit. It is merely an option, and the key to feeling and being free is keeping as many options open as possible.

If you have highly appreciated capital gain assets, such as a business, real estate, or stocks that you may want to sell in order to support your retirement, there are plenty of strategies for deferring the capital gains tax you'd have to pay. But you could completely and permanently reduce taxes, and even avoid them altogether.

Charitable Remainder Trusts

In this next strategy, you can even create a tax deduction through a charitable remainder trust. When you donate to a charitable remainder trust, a portion of your donation is tax deductible.

For example, if you sold an asset with $1 million in capital gains, you'd have to pay anywhere from $200,000 to $300,000 in taxes depending on the state you live in. This would leave you with around $700,000. To avoid capital gains taxes, you could place the asset in a charitable remainder trust and donate it to the charity of your choice. This could be any 501(c)(3), like a university, church, or charity. You avoid tax on the sale of the asset and get the partial tax deduction because when you die, the remaining value goes to charity.

At first glance, it appears that this would disinherit your family. However, if you have a death benefit, it acts as a permission slip allowing you to make the donation, save the tax, get the partial tax deduction, *and* have cash flow for the rest of your life. You're the first beneficiary; the charity is the second. The goal is to leave at least 10% to the charity when you die.

The Rockefeller Method begins thirty days after each child is born. The insurance is implemented long before the charitable trust decision. Those who already have a death benefit in force, are able to take the maximum cash flow from the charitable trust, just like the pension maximization example above. The death benefit replenishes your trust tax-free, especially if the insurance is owned in the proper trust. Now your family has life insurance inside of the trust both to borrow from and to replenish the money from charitable remainder trusts, paydown strategies, or reverse mortgages.

With the Rockefeller Method, you can both spend more money while you're alive *and* be more charitable. You get to give your money away, spend more money, and replenish the trust with life insurance. Spend, give, replenish, repeat. The Rockefellers have been implementing and integrating these types of strategies in their family for generations.

Typically, generational wealth lasts about two generations before all the money is spent. However, the Rockefeller Method is a way to ensure that your wealth continues far beyond that. The death benefit can replenish the trust when one generation utilizes the money. Even in the case of mistakes or market fluctuations, the death benefit becomes a contingency plan for replenishing the trust.

This allows you to pass down generational wealth and also create a value system for your kids, your grandkids, your great-grandkids, and so on. Your heirs that you never meet will know your name. Through the Family Constitution, they will know your values and what you stand for. You can change the destiny of your family by utilizing these policies properly, all while living your life to the fullest in your later years.

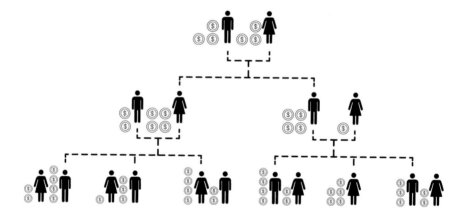

Properly structured, optimally funded whole life, combined with your Family Constitution and board of trustees, is the way to leave a financial legacy, empower your children, and share more of your human life value with them to help ensure that the wealth you leave is a blessing and not a curse.

Buy Your Net Worth

A lot of people think that net worth is the greatest indicator and measure of wealth. But the value of net worth is vastly overpromoted and overemphasized. Every business owner knows that if you can't access your net worth in times of need, it's relatively worthless. If you can't access your money, it doesn't count for much.

If you want net worth that you can actually access, then I'll tell you something that may surprise you: You don't want to *build* your net worth. You want to *buy* it.

So many people spend so much time worrying about accumulation and building a nest egg. The mantra is scrimp, save, and sacrifice to a net worth. But where do you put your money? How much risk do you take? How much time will it require?

Instead, you can create a nest egg right here, right now, through an optimally funded whole life insurance policy with a death benefit. If you buy a whole life insurance policy with a guaranteed $5 million death benefit, you've instantly added $5 million to your future balance sheet. When you die, your heirs will inherit at least $5 million.

How much money would you have to save to build a $5 million nest egg? How many market swings would you have to survive? How much would you have to risk? How many fees would you have to pay? How much time, effort, stress, and worry would you have to endure to make it all happen?

Unfortunately, when people get to retirement, they often don't have the lifestyle they'd hoped for. Between all the moving targets with interest rates, taxes, inflation, and the markets, it can feel impossible to navigate. It is difficult to predict what your net worth will be when you retire. There is one thing that's certain and predictable, though: death. By purchasing a death benefit through whole life insurance, you have a future sum of money that's contractually guaranteed from day one. You know the money will be there in the future.

Buying your net worth also has another major advantage over building your net worth: You can do it right now. Building your net worth takes time. But if you're older and don't have as much time, you can buy your net worth instead. You can secure an income tax-free asset that can be passed on to the next generation. *And* you can access your net worth and utilize that asset to live fully in your later years, Rockefeller style.

I remember meeting with my grandma when she was about seventy years old. She and my grandfather were angry because they had reached that age where you had a required minimum distribution on the 401(k). It was the first time I heard my grandma say the f-word (although not the last).

I recommended that they systematically take the money out of the 401(k) and place it into a whole life policy instead. The result was that when my grandmother died, an extra $250,000 was left tax-free to her five kids—six times more than the value of their home. Even better, they were able to live out their last years without worrying about whether the market was up or down. They were able to access and utilize their net worth to live fully, happily, and with the certainty that they wouldn't run out of money or leave nothing behind for their children.

I referred some clients to my coauthor and Whole Life Certified specialist, Michael Isom. They were approaching retirement within four years. These clients had "bought term and invested the difference." By the time Michael met with them, they had no life insurance because they felt like they were "self-insured." They planned to retire with their assets providing an income. However, they didn't want to take any risk whatsoever on their retirement savings. They planned to allocate it to a bond-type portfolio when they retired, which they were hoping would yield 5%.

The couple quickly learned that they could buy their net worth with a whole life policy that was funded to match their goals for retirement. This new death benefit permitted them to put a large portion of their retirement savings into a special guaranteed annuity that gave them 7% a year guaranteed, almost 300% more spendable income. All the while, the new death benefit guaranteed the surviving spouse the same amount of income, essentially buying their net worth.

When you buy your net worth, you create and insure your future. The death benefit increases income opportunity for your existing assets, helps with wealth capture and wealth creation, and means you can stop gambling and putting money toward things that don't make sense. Whole life allows you to buy your net worth and know with confidence that the money is there. It's secure.

Don't let all the money go away in one generation. You worked hard for this, and it's time for you to live a life you love. You don't get a second chance to create a legacy that lasts.

CHAPTER 7

The Most Certain Type of Insurance

There are many options for saving and storing your money. So why do I focus so much on properly structured, optimally funded whole life insurance? What makes it so much better than the alternatives like savings accounts, money markets, bonds, and the other types of life insurance that are available?

There is only one method of saving money that has survived for over a hundred years, that has lasted through the Great Depression, the 2008 recession, and the pandemic, and is still going strong today: whole life insurance.

TYPES OF LIFE INSURANCE

There are two main categories of life insurance: term insurance, which covers you for a limited period (or term), and permanent insurance, which covers you for the entirety of your life.

If you don't know what kind of life insurance to get, you don't understand the options, and you don't plan on reading the rest of this book, term insurance is probably your best bet—at least for now. Term is merely a stopgap to maximize your death benefit as you get your cash flow in order. But it's not the best long-term strategy.

Term Life Insurance

Term insurance is basically a bet: policyholder versus insurance company. The policyholder is betting on a death (their own, usually); the insurance company is betting on survival. If the insured person does not die in the allotted time, or "term," they lose all the payments they have made.

Policyholders make this bet hoping that they will lose. (And given that 98.9% of term life insurance premiums are lost, it's a pretty safe bet.) So why do they make it? Because it's cheap and they know their families will be financially protected when they die. So term policies are the most popular type of life insurance policy today, with ten- or twenty-year term policies being the most common.

Term insurance can be problematic for several reasons. First, the cost of term insurance becomes prohibitively expensive over a person's lifetime. If a thirty-year-old buys term insurance, their rates may be more than ten times the original premium when that term expires. When you are most likely to need it, it becomes too expensive. Indeed, by the time a person reaches the latter years of their retirement, they may find that their term premium payments exceed their death benefit!

If you look beyond the low price of term insurance's early years, you'll find that, when considered over an entire lifetime, it's actually one of the most expensive types of insurance on the market. It has a low initial price but a very high long-term cost for those who live longer.

Whole Life Insurance

Whole life insurance policies provide all the benefits I have discussed, which you can take advantage of throughout your lifetime: the ability to utilize cash value, tax protection, disability protection, long-term care replacement, and lawsuit protection.

Term insurance, on the other hand, carries no cash value within the policy and has no tangible living benefits. Moreover, properly structured, optimally funded whole life policies provide that priceless asset: certainty. And that certainty can make you more productive in all areas of your life.

Unlike term insurance, whole life insurance is not a gamble. Whole life insurance is designed to remain in force until the insured person dies, and there is a 100% chance that the insured person will die. Even if we find a way to live forever or extend life by decades, policies mature at age 100 or 120. Therefore, you have a "living death" and payout at those ages if you choose.

If you buy a $1 million permanent life insurance policy, the insurance company is guaranteed to pay out the $1 million (or more) someday unless you cancel the policy.

To make this payout, the insurance company collects money from you in the form of premiums while you are alive and invests that money.

Whole life insurance is not an investment. It acts more like a savings account: somewhere you put your money and utilize the cash value when opportunities arise. But it also comes with even more benefits, such as tax advantages, dividends, a death benefit, and liability protection.

Another benefit is the privacy of insurance. Whole life insurance is really the only private financial contract left to us today. Unlike bank accounts, brokerage accounts, or 401(k)s, there is no public record of life insurance contracts. Today, advisors purchase lists to market to people with money in accounts that are not private.

OTHER TYPES OF CASH VALUE INSURANCE

Whole life isn't the only type of cash value insurance. The other two main types are universal life (indexed and fixed) and variable universal life.

Universal Life Insurance

Essentially, universal life is optimally funded term insurance with a cash value. Universal life policies include an annual, renewable term insurance policy bundled with a savings or investment component.

Universal life policies have flexible premiums and adjustable death benefits. The rate at which the cash value in these policies grows is determined by the insurance company and based primarily on fixed income rates. This means that the insurance company can change both the rate of return and the cost of the insurance—which can result in predatory practices. The increase in the cost of insurance and the lower interest rates that are possible in a universal life policy can easily result in an increased premium or a lapse in coverage. If coverage does lapse, the policyholder may not only lose the policy but also end up having to pay taxes on any growth in cash value.

Ideally, what happens with a universal life policy is that the investment portion eventually increases enough to lower your net amount at risk, with leftover money helping to fund your retirement. While it does provide some tax advantages over term insurance, you may still end up having to pay higher and higher premiums as you age or face the chance of a policy lapsing and potentially creating a taxable event.

Since the insurance is annual, renewable term insurance, it can increase in cost every year. Each year, more of your premiums may go toward the life insurance and less toward the investment. If the market is not performing well or other conditions are not ideal, policyholders often end up paying bigger premiums in later years to keep their policies going.

The death benefit in universal life policies is also not guaranteed—unless you are willing to potentially pay higher premiums, since their cost is not fixed. You can add a guaranteed death benefit rider to your policy. But if you miss a payment or, in some cases, borrow against your cash value, those riders may be negated and the guarantee voided. So universal life policies can work, but carry unnecessary risk unless you pay back the money you borrow, never miss a premium payment, or never borrow against your cash value.

It's important to note that indexed universal life (IUL), equity-indexed universal life (EIUL), and variable universal life (VUL) insurance policies are not savings vehicles. They are investments. This is where your clarity is vital. Do you know your Investor DNA? Are you clear about what is a healthy investment for you versus just gambling? Invest, yes, but don't gamble.

Variable Universal Life Insurance

The first life insurance policy I ever bought when I was eighteen years old was a VUL. Yeah, what a weirdo—I bought insurance when I was eighteen, before I was even married. I was trying to invest for the future, and with a small amount of money in a small town, this was what I was offered.

A VUL has a cash value that is invested in market subaccounts and has adjustable premiums and death benefits. The subaccounts vary with market performance, hence the name "variable." Essentially, it is a universal life policy with the added opportunity to invest in the stock market.

Here's the problem with VULs: Unless you understand the market and plan on actively managing those subaccounts, you'll be more of a gambler than an investor. And even if you understand the market, you'll still have to deal with the additional complexity of the VUL due to the expenses of the policy and increased costs against the policy in a down market.

A VUL offers limited stability and almost no control over your returns. This is a tool that chases market returns and is less useful for storing cash and leveraging living benefits. It would not be an alternative to your savings account and would actually compete with your retirement plan. The performance is jeopardized not only by a variable market, but also by variable insurance costs, especially during losing market years.

Declines in the market can be hazardous and increase the cost of insurance—which the policyholder must pay for, usually by selling off shares of their subaccounts. Of course, a market decline would mean shares are worth less, which means the policyholder would have to sell even more shares.

When I purchased a VUL, I was told that if it earned 18%, annualized and compounded for forty years, a mere seventy dollars a month could make me a multimillionaire. What I very quickly learned was that the success rate for this scenario was approximately *no chance in hell*. It wasn't long before I started calling it "Very Ugly Life" instead of "variable universal life." According to my economics thesis in college, VULs had a 97.8% failure rate at the minimums I was funding mine.

If your subaccounts go down in value, your net risk goes up (insurance death benefit minus your cash value), your average share value goes down, and the cost of insurance goes up. VUL insurance exposes you to the risk of the market, which in turn exposes you to the rising cost of insurance. You have no guarantees because you may have to pay a higher and higher premium to keep your death benefit, all while your cash value is decreasing. There's no guarantee of earning interest and no guarantee on your cash value because expenses can take from your cash value. It's an incredibly high-risk policy.

This information is hard to come by if you talk to people who sell VULs. Their illustrations and proposals typically show a much higher rate of return. Why? Because they either don't show volatility (market ups and downs) or they do show much higher returns than occur in the market. Or both.

Too many variables can destroy these projected numbers in a moment. Fortunately, my pain is your gain. You invested in this book and can learn the easy way. And if you are already in a VUL structure, a Whole Life Certified agent can discuss options with you.

GET THE MOST CERTAINTY WITH WHOLE LIFE

If you want certainty, it's much better to have fewer moving pieces. That's where whole life insurance comes in. Whole life is not as flashy on paper as indexed universal life or variable universal life. The contracts are also much shorter because they are less complicated with fewer moving pieces.

People are led to believe that high returns only come with high risks, so words like "guarantee" and "low risk" make some people think only of low returns. But the truth is that certainty, when understood and utilized, has huge economic value. Don't think of this as an investment, but rather as a key component to the Rockefeller Method, an alternative to bank accounts and fixed-income debt instruments like bonds, and a way to help ensure your value and legacy.

Whole life gives you control and certainty, and it transfers more risk than any other life insurance contract. With a universal or variable universal policy, the insured person takes on more risk when conditions change. With whole life, the insurance company takes on that risk.

A whole life insurance contract is a unilateral contract, meaning that once you have it and know what your terms are, the insurance company can't change them on you even if your health or the company's situation change. The insurance company is contractually bound to honor the promise they made to you up front.

Whole life provides more certainty than any other life insurance contract. It gives you a guaranteed minimum interest rate, premiums that are guaranteed never to go up, a guaranteed death benefit, guaranteed cash value, and guaranteed access to that cash value. Your existing cash value is not impacted by market fluctuations. Even if you miss a payment, the guarantees are not negated. The premium is taken from the cash value and the death benefit remains guaranteed.

Along with that certainty come tangible economic benefits during your lifetime. With some simple calculations, it's easy to see how utilizing whole life—and using the cash value—as the centerpiece of your wealth infrastructure and savings strategy can outperform the "buy term and invest the difference" strategy. Check out Appendix 1 to see exactly how these calculations can play out. Whole life gives you a permission slip to spend your assets, freeing you from the captivity of living off interest alone. It gives you the ability to spend more and enjoy more as you age. And it gives you the certainty of knowing versus hoping, which has far-reaching benefits across all areas of your life, economic and otherwise. These benefits can also reach beyond your life and into the lives of your descendants, just as they have with the Rockefellers.

PROTECT YOUR PEACE OF MIND

 Life insurance is a permission slip to live in the abundance mindset because you know that your finances are settled. This peace of mind will allow you to produce at an even higher level than before. This is something called the certainty of maximization, or the economic value of certainty.

Protection leads to production, not just in terms of earning money, but in terms of your quality of life. That peace of mind will translate into clarity, joy, and the mental space and creativity that allows you to generate and produce more. This higher production and quality of life that awaits you will more than pay for the increased coverage.

People often think you either have to invest or protect. The good news is, we don't live in a world of either/or. We live in a world of abundance. It's possible to have the maximum amount of insurance without hurting your net worth or your cash flow.

Plug financial leaks, fund your cash value policy, and utilize the cash for the right opportunities along the way. Save on tax, save on term insurance, and protect your cash from volatile markets and financial predators. This is what the wealthy do.

CHAPTER 8

But Dave Ramsey and Suze Orman Said No!

When it comes to getting financial train wrecks back on track or building the necessary mindfulness around money, there are probably no better financial pundits than Dave Ramsey and Suze Orman. However, when it comes to building true generational wealth, their advice is both limited and flawed. The Rockefellers don't take advice from Dave and Suze. And unless you are in a dire situation or a financial train wreck, neither should you.

Given that Dave and Suze both scorn permanent life insurance products, you may be raising your eyebrows at our whole life insurance recommendation. There is a lot of misinformation about it out there, and terribly designed policies that reinforce the stigma. I even once heard someone refer to whole life insurance as "a hole you throw your money into."

Ramsey has said that "cash value life insurance is one of the worst financial products available."

Orman put whole life insurance in her top ten list of hated investments because "they literally do nothing for you, and do everything, in my opinion, for the financial salesperson that sold them to you."

Their advice, like so many typical advisors, is to "buy term and invest the difference."

Then why do I say the opposite? Are Dave and Suze just plain wrong? Well, not exactly.

Ramsey and Orman both believe in cutting back, budgeting and sacrificing, and not spending too much. If the road to wealth is being price-conscious and spending less, in that context they are right. In the short term, term life insurance has a significantly lower price tag than whole life insurance.

However, I'm not interested in helping you nickel-and-dime in the short term. I'm interested in helping you create economic independence and stability in the long term, with maximum options for the rest of your life. From that perspective, Dave and Suze couldn't be more wrong about whole life insurance.

According to Ramsey and Orman, financial advisors who sell whole life insurance sell these products solely to benefit themselves rather than you, the client. In some cases, that's exactly what's happening. Some insurance agents *do* oversell underfunded permanent life insurance policies to get their commissions. But poor practices by a few salesmen who are either uninformed or greedy—as they oversell the commissionable aspect of the policy and undersell the paid up additions (PUA)—do not devalue the merit of optimally funded whole life insurance.

Find a Whole Life Certified specialist trained in the Rockefeller Method and proper policy design at wholelifecertified.com. This product is merely a vehicle for storing your cash that can be utilized due to its unique nature and its features that are otherwise unavailable. It's about setting up your policy correctly, minimizing the commission, and maximizing the benefits and efficiency for the policyholder—you.

The truth is that the mutual funds Suze and Dave recommend over whole life insurance have fees that compound over time to be higher than the insurance commissions. As Jack Bogle, the founder of Vanguard, famously said, "What happens in the mutual fund business is that the magic of compound interest on returns is overwhelmed by the tyranny of compounding costs. It's a mathematical fact."

But Ramsey and Orman defend their positions on loaded mutual funds. Fee-based advisors who sell 401(k)s not only get a percentage of what is in the account every year; they can also sell their book of business for twelve to fifteen times EBITA (earnings before interest, taxes, depreciation, and amortization. That's a huge return (commission).

Dave and Suze focus on scrimping and saving via budgeting, which leads them to give very generic and limiting advice on what you can do with your money. The risky claims financial gurus make come after the money is saved and the advice turns to investing. Dave Ramsey claims that you can get 10–12% returns investing in a mutual fund. However, the vast majority of mutual funds don't get anywhere close to that.

Moreover, there isn't any sense in comparing mutual funds to whole life insurance. Using properly structured, optimally funded whole life as the foundation of your Rockefeller Method strategy isn't an investment. It's not an either/or. You can access the money from your whole life insurance policy to fund any investment opportunity that will yield you 12%.

Storing your cash in a whole life insurance policy is not the be-all, end-all of your portfolio. This is a place to store your medium-term money. Getting amazing returns isn't even the primary reason to store your cash in whole life. It simply allows you to become more flexible with your money. It gives you a solid and stable foundation while doing much better than a savings account—all while having tax efficiencies as well. If you look at strategy and integration, whole life insurance makes sense. If you look at it as an individual, isolated product that means you merely leave money behind when you die, you miss the power and cash flow that it can unlock.

Another strange claim Dave Ramsey has made against whole life insurance is that the savings you build up don't go to your family when you die. This shows a great misunderstanding of how whole life works. As long as you pay your premiums, you guarantee that your family will receive the money. If you get a $5 million whole life policy and pay your premiums, you guarantee that your estate will receive that $5 million. The number will increase as your dividends are paid and the value of your cash increases.

Michael Does the Math

Assuming you pay your premiums, whole life is guaranteed to pay out to your beneficiaries and your cash value will grow. But with whole life, you can even stop paying premiums at some point. You can do this using one of two main options: a feature called "reduced paid-up" (RPU), and another called "premium offset."

At any point during the policy contract, you can exercise the reduced paid-up option. This means you reduce the death benefit to the point that it is "paid up." It's best to do this after seven years or more of holding the policy, but it can be done even before that. This option is irreversible, however, so you want to make the decision carefully.

Once you've paid up, the cash value is in the policy and will continue to grow along with the death benefit, and they will equal each other at the end of the term of the whole life policy, age 121. (All whole life policies are designed this way.) Once you opt for an RPU, there is still a small cost to cover in the policy each year. However, the policy more than pays for itself at this point. You have elected to lower the amount of your death benefit, thus lowering your cost of insurance and making it as efficient as possible with the internal rate of return on the cash value.

Premium offset gives you the ability to use the cash value growth year by year, with the dividends paying the base annual premium into the policy. The cash value and death benefit will not grow as quickly because you don't pay into the policy out of pocket. However, it will continue to grow.

This option can be turned on and off during the life of the policy. We like to use this option if a client is not 100%

sure they want to stop altogether. For example, what if they still have some investments to liquidate and want a place to save that cash? Having the option to continue to pay into the whole life policy would be valuable.

Saving money in whole life this way keeps your money guaranteed, protected, and liquid.

The following chart shows a client paying $36,000 per

year into a whole life policy for twenty years. At the end of this period, the client has $1,089,453 in cash value. At that point, they take the reduced paid-up option and stop making payments. They reduce the death benefit to the point at which the policy is paid up (calculated by the life insurance company upon request).

Year	Age	Total Premium	Dividend	Premium Outlay	Cum. Premium Outlay	Total Cash Value	Change in Total Cash Value	Change in CV Less Prem. Outlay	Total Death Benefit w/out Div	Total Death Benefit
1	30	36,000	357	36,000	36,000	25,682	25,682	-10,318	1,261,826	1,262,183
2	31	36,000	1,042	36,000	72,000	54,221	28,539	-7,461	1,367,184	1,368,226
3	32	36,000	1,786	36,000	108,000	86,373	32,152	-3,848	1,472,440	1,474,226
4	33	36,000	2,579	36,000	144,000	123,490	37,117	1,117	1,577,759	1,580,339
5	34	36,000	4,155	36,000	180,000	164,364	40,874	4,874	1,683,259	1,687,414
6	35	36,000	5,275	36,000	216,000	206,184	41,820	5,820	1,789,074	1,794,348
7	36	36,000	6,480	36,000	252,000	250,362	44,177	8,177	1,895,356	1,901,835
8	37	36,000	7,754	36,000	288,000	296,982	46,620	10,620	2,002,199	2,009,953
9	38	36,000	9,099	36,000	324,000	346,165	49,183	13,183	2,109,768	2,118,867
10	39	36,000	10,505	36,000	360,000	398,017	51,852	15,852	2,218,178	2,228,683
11	40	36,000	12,077	36,000	396,000	452,425	54,408	18,408	2,327,543	2,339,620
12	41	36,000	13,724	36,000	432,000	509,791	57,367	21,367	2,438,003	2,451,727
13	42	36,000	15,441	36,000	468,000	570,266	60,474	24,474	2,549,783	2,565,223
14	43	36,000	17,162	36,000	504,000	633,943	63,677	27,677	2,662,958	2,680,120
15	44	36,000	18,908	36,000	540,000	701,074	67,131	31,131	2,777,453	2,796,362
16	45	36,000	20,760	36,000	576,000	770,860	69,785	33,785	2,893,238	2,913,998
17	46	36,000	22,688	36,000	612,000	844,379	73,519	37,519	3,010,402	3,033,090
18	47	36,000	24,705	36,000	648,000	921,840	77,461	41,461	3,128,991	3,153,696
19	48	36,000	26,806	36,000	684,000	1,003,454	81,614	45,614	3,249,044	3,275,850
20	49	36,000	29,030	36,000	720,000	1,089,453	85,999	49,999	3,370,592	3,399,622
21 [1]	50	0	30,235	0	720,000	1,147,748	58,295	58,295	2,748,662	2,778,897
22	51	0	31,787	0	720,000	1,209,022	61,274	61,274	2,823,029	2,854,816
23	52	0	33,457	0	720,000	1,273,490	64,467	64,467	2,899,256	2,932,713
24	53	0	35,224	0	720,000	1,341,290	67,800	67,800	2,977,481	3,012,704
25	54	0	37,121	0	720,000	1,412,602	71,312	71,312	3,057,781	3,094,902

You'll notice that the client still earns a rate of return within the policy after their premium payments have stopped. The first year after making payments, the cash value jumped from $1,089,453 to $1,147,748—a 5.35% internal rate of return (and on a tax-free basis, let me remind you)!

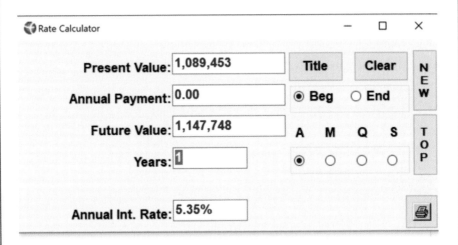

It's one thing to earn a great tax-free rate of return while we are accumulating wealth. It's quite another to earn it when we are no longer trading time for money! How great to have this amount of money someplace during "retirement" that pays you over 5% a year tax-free. Unheard of. Furthermore, you have the death benefit to leverage against all of your other assets on a paydown, permission-slip basis.

SHOULD YOU "BUY TERM AND INVEST THE DIFFERENCE"?

Ramsey and Orman promote the "buy term and invest the difference" strategy over whole life. Their advice is to buy the lower premium term insurance and invest the difference in a mutual fund or some other investment vehicle.

Fee-based advisors also love this strategy because the premiums on term insurance are so much lower than those on permanent insurance, especially in the early years. They make money on assets under management and may not sell insurance. They may not be educated about insurance, just as many insurance agents don't have the same level of expertise with investments and may therefore only focus on insurance.

If you follow this advice from Ramsey, Orman, and other financial gurus, you will run into more problems. If you live anywhere close to life expectancy, your insurance will not pay out. In many cases, your investments will not be protected from creditors. Your liquid savings will be taxable, and those have grown at anemic rates for most of the last two decades. If you get sued, your mutual funds will likely be up for grabs. You will have to pay taxes on your gains from mutual funds. And even if you protect your money in a 401(k) or traditional IRA, those accounts are subject to future income tax. Plus, they are sitting ducks for the estate tax.

Here's the problem with this shortsighted, binary strategy: Let's say you buy a thirty-year term insurance policy with a $1 million death benefit. Your goal is to maintain this death benefit for thirty years, invest the difference, and then cancel the term insurance. The interest rate you would have to make on your investment to match what you would make using a properly structured, optimally funded whole life policy would be a whopping 9.8%. It is highly unlikely that you will find that percentage when investing, especially considering it would need to be safe, stable, and liquid, and the return would have to be net after fees.

Michael Does the Math

Let's dive deeper into that 9.8% interest rate I mentioned above. First, let's get on the same page with how an average rate of return is calculated. We know that to get that average, we add up the numbers and then divide them by the number of years.

This chart shows an extreme example to make the point. Let's suppose you invest $100, and it gains 100% in the first year. You have a $100 gain for $200 total. However, in the second year, your rate of return is –50%, taking you back down to $100 total. The next year you get a 100% rate of return, followed by another year with a –50% return.

If you add up our four years of returns, 100 – 50 + 100 – 50, then divide by four, you get an average annual return of 25%. But you have actually earned a net 0%. Which is most useful? Average or actual? Actual, obviously.

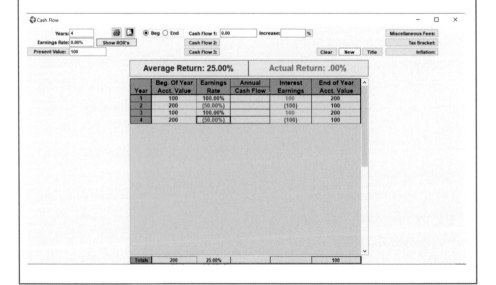

Between 1993 and 2012, the S&P 500, reinvesting dividends, averaged 9.92%. This is why the 9-10% average rate of return is so commonly cited by money managers.

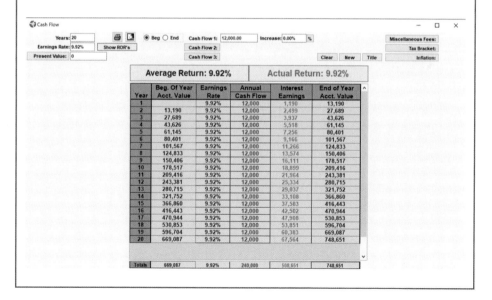

Market History — □ ×

First Year: 1993 Present Value: [ ] Annual Payment: [ ]
Last Year: 2012   DJ-NoDiv | S&P-NoDiv | S&P-Div | DJ-Bond | T-Bond | T-Note | T-Bill   Source: Pinnacle Data Corp.

AVERAGE ROR:	8.36%	7.86%	9.92%	6.04%	5.08%	3.83%	3.22%
Year	Dow Jones Ind. NO Dividends	S&P 500 NO Dividends	S&P 500 With Dividends	Dow Jones Comp. Bond	10 Year U.S. T-Bond	5 Year U.S. T-Note	1 Year U.S. T-Bill
1993	13.52	7.06	9.98	1.01	6.27	4.38	3.60
1994	2.18	(1.54)	1.32	(10.65)	7.85	7.77	7.12
1995	34.88	34.11	37.20	12.53	6.12	5.50	5.30
1996	24.43	20.26	22.70	(5.83)	6.63	6.07	5.51
1997	23.63	31.01	33.12	11.65	5.96	5.72	5.49
1998	15.31	26.69	28.38	9.69	5.16	4.62	4.63
1999	23.66	19.51	20.87	(3.39)	6.46	6.28	5.35
2000	(6.26)	(10.14)	(9.07)	11.02	5.43	5.07	5.71
2001	(5.38)	(13.04)	(11.85)	9.29	5.49	4.07	2.23
2002	(14.55)	(23.37)	(21.98)	10.61	5.10	2.63	1.43
2003	20.94	26.38	28.45	10.35	5.10	2.79	1.27
2004	3.07	8.99	10.87	7.00	4.84	3.40	2.71
2005	1.10	3.00	4.92	1.33	4.71	4.39	4.37
2006	15.00	13.62	15.68	3.94	4.82	4.59	4.96
2007	4.56	3.53	5.51	5.00	4.58	3.35	3.28
2008	(30.74)	(38.49)	(36.63)	1.80	3.04	1.16	0.45
2009	17.15	23.45	25.85	17.85	4.53	2.00	0.41
2010	10.27	12.78	14.89	8.44	4.23	1.54	0.30
2011	6.23	(0.00)	2.23	8.32	2.63	0.65	0.12
2012	8.19	13.41	16.00	10.88	2.56	0.57	0.15

Let's take that 9.92% average and use it for this next, future value calculation and assume that you add $12,000 a year to an account for twenty years. Assuming you also get a steady 9.92% rate of return every year, your contributions should compound to a total of $748,651.

Cash Flow — □ ×

Years: 20   ● Beg ○ End Cash Flow 1: 12,000.00 Increase: 0.00% %   Miscellaneous Fees: [ ]
Earnings Rate: 9.92% Show ROR's   Cash Flow 2: [ ]   Tax Bracket: [ ]
Present Value: 0   Cash Flow 3: [ ]   Clear | New | Title   Inflation: [ ]

	Average Return: 9.92%			Actual Return: 9.92%	
Year	Beg. Of Year Acct. Value	Earnings Rate	Annual Cash Flow	Interest Earnings	End of Year Acct. Value
1		9.92%	12,000	1,190	13,190
2	13,190	9.92%	12,000	2,499	27,689
3	27,689	9.92%	12,000	3,937	43,626
4	43,626	9.92%	12,000	5,518	61,145
5	61,145	9.92%	12,000	7,256	80,401
6	80,401	9.92%	12,000	9,166	101,567
7	101,567	9.92%	12,000	11,266	124,833
8	124,833	9.92%	12,000	13,574	150,406
9	150,406	9.92%	12,000	16,111	178,517
10	178,517	9.92%	12,000	18,899	209,416
11	209,416	9.92%	12,000	21,964	243,381
12	243,381	9.92%	12,000	25,334	280,715
13	280,715	9.92%	12,000	29,037	321,752
14	321,752	9.92%	12,000	33,108	366,860
15	366,860	9.92%	12,000	37,583	416,443
16	416,443	9.92%	12,000	42,502	470,944
17	470,944	9.92%	12,000	47,908	530,853
18	530,853	9.92%	12,000	53,851	596,704
19	596,704	9.92%	12,000	60,383	669,087
20	669,087	9.92%	12,000	67,564	748,651
Totals	669,087	9.92%	240,000	508,651	748,651

However, we know that investments don't work this way. Investments fluctuate over time—an *average* rate of return is not the same as an *actual* rate of return. Unfortunately, far too many advisors project steady, year-after-year rates of return.

We also have to account for fees charged to you on managed money. In his book *Money: Master the Game*, Tony Robbins shows total management fees as high as 3.5–4% of the entire account balance, annually. For our illustration, we'll use a conservative 2% management fee. Calculating for fees, you now have a net 7.72% actual rate of return.

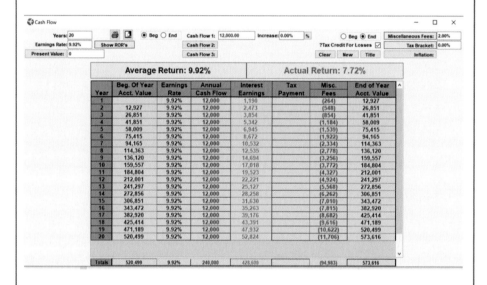

But now, instead of showing a steady annual 9.92% return, let's use the actual market history. In this case, you're left with an actual rate of return of 4.13%, and you're earning that meager return with a lot of risk and uncertainty.

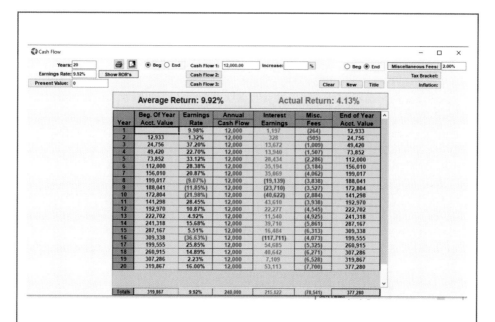

	Average Return: 9.92%			Actual Return: 4.13%		
Year	Beg. Of Year Acct. Value	Earnings Rate	Annual Cash Flow	Interest Earnings	Misc. Fees	End of Year Acct. Value
1		9.98%	12,000	1,197	(264)	12,933
2	12,933	1.32%	12,000	328	(505)	24,756
3	24,756	37.20%	12,000	13,672	(1,009)	49,420
4	49,420	22.70%	12,000	13,940	(1,507)	73,852
5	73,852	33.12%	12,000	28,434	(2,286)	112,000
6	112,000	28.38%	12,000	35,194	(3,184)	156,010
7	156,010	20.87%	12,000	35,069	(4,062)	199,017
8	199,017	(9.07%)	12,000	(19,139)	(3,838)	188,041
9	188,041	(11.85%)	12,000	(23,710)	(3,527)	172,804
10	172,804	(21.98%)	12,000	(40,622)	(2,884)	141,298
11	141,298	28.45%	12,000	43,610	(3,938)	192,970
12	192,970	10.87%	12,000	22,277	(4,545)	222,702
13	222,702	4.92%	12,000	11,540	(4,925)	241,318
14	241,318	15.68%	12,000	39,710	(5,861)	287,167
15	287,167	5.51%	12,000	16,464	(6,313)	309,338
16	309,338	(36.63%)	12,000	(117,711)	(4,073)	199,555
17	199,555	25.85%	12,000	54,685	(5,325)	260,915
18	260,915	14.89%	12,000	40,642	(6,271)	307,286
19	307,286	2.23%	12,000	7,109	(6,528)	319,867
20	319,867	16.00%	12,000	53,113	(7,700)	377,280
Totals	319,867	9.92%	240,000	215,822	(78,541)	377,280

This doesn't even account for human nature, which tells us that people don't stay invested for this long. Typically, they react emotionally to market conditions and get in and out of investments quickly.

Term policies are designed specifically to be dropped, with the assumption that once a person retires, they will have plenty of assets with which to care for themselves; their kids will be grown and financially independent; and they will no longer have any income, so they won't need income replacement coverage. This is what is commonly known as being "self-insured."

To be "self-insured" is a fallacy—a person is either insured or not. Moreover, a person doesn't cease to have human life value just because their employment income stops. Term insurance is focused solely on protecting income rather than human life value. The truth is, the more assets a person creates, the more likely it is that they will want the protection of insurance (just like the Rockefellers). At that point, insurance moves from income replacement to asset and legacy insurance. (For a more detailed explanation of this concept, see my book, *Killing Sacred Cows 2.0*.)

Many fee-based advisors would respond to this by saying that a person can create even more assets by investing the money they would have spent on a permanent policy in products that have a higher rate of return. Investments could indeed yield higher returns; you could potentially get 10–12% on real estate or during certain periods in the stock market, while the guarantees and dividends on a whole life policy are lower.

However, these numbers alone don't take the whole picture into account. If you bought a thirty-year term policy for $750 a year and then dropped it after the term, you would have spent $22,500 on premiums. You are never getting that money back. What's more, you lost the additional interest you could have made on that money had you saved it. Even worse, you also lost the amount of the death benefit you dropped. And depending on your situation, you may not be able to qualify for insurance coverage again, so you may have lost your chance of having a death benefit at all.

Buying term and investing the difference could be compared to whole life and investing the cash value. But there are times when it might not make sense to invest, and in these times, whole life provides certainty and dividends.

Of course, the question most people have is, "What's the use of saving my money like this if I only get it back after I'm dead?" But again, the truth is that you can use the money accumulating in your policy any time you want. Unlike term life insurance, where your premium money is gone forever, the premium money you put into a whole life insurance policy is still yours to use while you are alive, and it will 100% certainly be returned to your beneficiaries after you die.

Investing and saving are not the same. One has volatility and risk, whereas the other features liquidity and stability. If you can get double-digit returns for extended periods, you will outperform your cash value. Yet with whole life, that cash value can be accessed when opportunities come along. Therefore, this is not an either/or situation. Nor is it a comparison. Whole life is an asset allocation choice you can use with some of your funds to protect your capital, lock in benefits, and enjoy access to that capital along the way.

Ramsay and Orman are focused primarily on spending less. But spending less can cost you more. And really, nobody hates insurance—they just hate paying for it. People see it as a necessary evil because they don't understand the benefits that insurance can provide. The best way to reduce insurance expenses is to buy as many of the right kinds as possible.

There are three ways to deal with risk: avoiding it, retaining it, or transferring it. If you retain your risk in order to reduce expenses, you will almost certainly end up paying more in the long run. The initial premium with whole life is much higher than the amount you would pay for term insurance, but it comes with much higher value in the form of benefits and guarantees—and it accumulates cash.

CONSIDER PRICE, COST, AND VALUE

If there were no cost to insurance, how much would you take? As much as they offered, right? Start with the amount that would be required to replace your income and therefore your economic value. Consider both price and cost.

Price is the premium you pay. Cost is the net impact considering cash value and benefits. If you only look at the price today, term insurance is the clear winner over whole life. But term can have a much higher cost over time. If you live to life expectancy, term insurance will cost more in premium paid than death benefit has in value. Only 1.1% of term policies pay out a death benefit. Therefore, 98.9% of premium dollars for term life insurance were essentially a temporary benefit to protect against something that did not occur. Low up-front price, high long-term cost.

Michael Does the Math

The following charts show a client starting with a twenty-year term life policy at age thirty-one. For the twenty-year term, the premiums are $540 per year for a total of $10,800 over the full term. When the term expires and the client is fifty-one, the premiums skyrocket to $10,200 per year!

That amount increases each year. If the client continues paying term premiums, by age seventy-seven they will have paid more in premiums than the policy is worth. And again, if the client were to drop the policy, all the premium dollars would be wasted.

Year	Age	Annualized Contract Premium	Guaranteed Death Benefit
1	31	540	1,000,000
2	32	540	1,000,000
3	33	540	1,000,000
4	34	540	1,000,000
5	35	540	1,000,000
6	36	540	1,000,000
7	37	540	1,000,000
8	38	540	1,000,000
9	39	540	1,000,000
10	40	540	1,000,000
11	41	540	1,000,000
12	42	540	1,000,000
13	43	540	1,000,000
14	44	540	1,000,000
15	45	540	1,000,000
16	46	540	1,000,000
17	47	540	1,000,000
18	48	540	1,000,000
19	49	540	1,000,000
20	50	540	1,000,000
21	51	10,200	1,000,000
22	52	10,960	1,000,000
23	53	11,910	1,000,000
24	54	13,030	1,000,000
25	55	14,200	1,000,000
26	56	15,370	1,000,000
27	57	16,450	1,000,000
28	58	17,490	1,000,000
29	59	18,570	1,000,000
30	60	19,830	1,000,000

Year	Age	Annualized Contract Premium	Guaranteed Death Benefit
36	66	35,890	1,000,000
37	67	39,720	1,000,000
38	68	43,810	1,000,000
39	69	48,360	1,000,000
40	70	53,490	1,000,000
41	71	59,520	1,000,000
42	72	66,210	1,000,000
43	73	74,180	1,000,000
44	74	83,390	1,000,000
45	75	93,830	1,000,000
46	76	105,360	1,000,000
47	77	117,890	1,000,000
48	78	131,550	1,000,000
49	79	146,530	1,000,000
50	80	163,500	1,000,000
51	81	182,980	1,000,000
52	82	205,640	1,000,000
53	83	230,780	1,000,000
54	84	259,860	1,000,000
55	85	293,340	1,000,000
56	86	332,000	1,000,000
57	87	376,430	1,000,000
58	88	427,150	1,000,000
59	89	483,990	1,000,000
60	90	544,950	1,000,000
61	91	609,140	1,000,000
62	92	674,070	1,000,000
63	93	737,870	1,000,000
64	94	799,770	1,000,000

When you drop your term insurance due to the increased premiums in later years, or your assets have grown and you choose to be "self-insured," there will be a much higher cost—even though you save on the premiums. The cost is the lack of access to your assets now acting as your insurance. What is the opportunity cost of what you can do with those funds if they aren't tied up acting as insurance?

Most people look only at the price of whole life insurance. And when it isn't properly structured and optimally funded, the cost *is* much higher and the value much lower.

When your properly structured, optimally funded whole life insurance comes with a permanent death benefit (one that lasts one day longer than you), there is an income tax-free payout to your family trust. Through dividends, your cash value is highly likely to be greater than your premium amount after a few years. You can access that cash value to capitalize on opportunities throughout your life. Higher price, lower cost.

Ask yourself: *If price weren't an issue, what tool would I want to protect my family and my human life value?* Plan your best-case economic value, the income you are currently earning, and how you can replace that value if something were to happen to you. If you died, would you want to leave your family in the same financial situation you are in now? A worse financial situation? How about an even better financial situation?

When you "buy your future net worth" in the form of the death benefit, the payout is guaranteed. You'll recover the cost of term insurance and gain tax efficiency. You will have dividends in the policy gain momentum to the point where you eventually beat the interest you'd earn in a savings account. Cash value in a permanent life insurance policy is comparable to a bond portfolio without the downside risk.

If all of this isn't enough, look no further than the Rockefellers. CPA Sheila Brandenberg worked in the Rockefeller Global Family Office. In an email discussing optimally funded whole life, she wrote to me, "Thankfully, many of the strategies you speak about I am aware of, and [they] are commonplace and a matter of course in those contexts." The Rockefellers themselves know that a strategy using whole life insurance is the way to go.

Client Spotlight from Michael

One of my clients, Tom, owns a small design and print company with five employees. He's married and has three kids. When I first met Tom, he viewed insurance as a "necessary evil."

After our thorough financial assessment, we discovered that Tom brought home $150,000 in annual income to his family. He had a $500,000 term life insurance policy for himself, but no life insurance policy for his wife.

I asked him, "If there was no cost for life insurance, how much would you want?"

"As much as I could get," Tom responded.

"And how much do you love your family?"

"They are everything to me. They are the reason I get up every day and hustle."

Tom admitted to me that he occasionally wondered if he had enough life insurance to take care of his family in the event of his death. "And yes, Michael," he told me, "if something happened to me, I would want them to be taken care of."

The first reason most of our clients want to purchase life insurance is love. They love their families and want to provide for them if they die unexpectedly.

When our business partners, Ray and Les, died in that plane crash in the summer of 2006, I called their spouses early that morning and woke them up to tell them what had happened. Both of them were pregnant at the time. That is not the kind of phone call I wish on anyone. Thank God Ray and Les each had the maximum death benefit. It did not replace them physically, but it did replace their income for their families.

When Tom came to me, he was forty-one years old. A $500,000 death benefit would not replace his $150,000 annual income for very long. Replacing it would actually take a $3 million death benefit—twenty times his current annual income—earning 5% interest.

I asked Tom, "Does $3 million seem like a big number?"

"Yes," he said. And it was, compared to the $500,000 he had in place at the time. However, the $3 million represents $150,000 per year of replacement income to his family.

I asked another question: "Are your dreams and goals the same for your family if you are here or not here?"

He answered, "Even more so if I am not here."

By insuring his full human life value, Tom would have the peace of mind of knowing—versus hoping—that his family would be okay in the event of his death.

But as you know, there are even more reasons to use whole life insurance. I told Tom, "Statistically speaking, if you are insurable today and don't have any major health concerns, your life expectancy is ninety-five. It's one thing to plan for an unexpected death. But we also have to plan for you to live a long life. The death benefit in a permanent whole life insurance policy can be spent by you and your wife while you are alive, and you can also leave it to your kids."

"Oh, come on," he protested. "That's unheard of. It sounds too good to be true."

I shared a basic example with him of how to spend down the death benefit with a reverse mortgage, which we'll discuss in greater detail in Chapter 8. I told him that my wife and I plan to do a reverse mortgage later in life. A reverse mortgage is an increasing line of credit against the value of your home that can be established after you reach the age of sixty-two. After that, the older you get, the more equity can be paid out to you; the value of the amount they will give you increases by an average of 8% a year. You can write off the mortgage interest that accrues on reverse mortgages. (The current law is up to $750,000. Consult with a tax expert for your specific circumstances.) This means it's tax-free retirement income.

When we have both passed, our trust can use the death benefit from our life insurance policies to pay off the reverse mortgage and keep the home—or not, and let the bank take it. There is no liability or obligation to pay it off.

This is just one way that the wealthy spend and enjoy more, tax-free, and leave it behind.

Helping Tom see this perspective created a desire in him to make a change. His only question then was, "When do we start?"

Dave Ramsey and Suze Orman are both smart people with great strengths. But they're both dogmatic about insurance. Plus, Dave needs a hug. Why is he so angry, as rich as he is?

The fears that Dave, Suze, and other financial pundits have about whole life insurance only apply to poorly designed policies. They don't apply to well-designed ones.

In the next chapters of this book, we'll discuss how to properly design a policy and the advantages it will create for your financial future.

CHAPTER 9

Design Your Plan Properly

The Rockefeller Method is far more than simply buying a whole life insurance policy. It's a comprehensive, coordinated plan that must be designed properly. Your whole life policy itself must also be structured properly.

However, not all policies are created equal, not all companies are equal, and not all agents are equal. Whole Life Certified specialists are trained in the Rockefeller Method and protocols that minimize commissions while maximizing your cash. They know how to integrate the strategies that lead to more cash in your pocket and your plan.

Find someone who will look at your entire financial architecture holistically to make sure that your optimally funded whole life policy fits in with your overall plan. And look for someone who uses these strategies as I describe them. We provide a list of the certified specialists that we recommend at wholelifecertified.com.

INSURE YOUR FULL HUMAN LIFE VALUE

To make optimally funded whole life break even on cash flow as quickly as possible, you get a low amount of insurance coverage and then optimally fund your policy as much as you can. However, fully protecting your human life value with the proper amount of death benefit is a top priority. It locks in opportunities for conversion and increasing your optimally funded whole life in the future. Before you even consider optimally funded whole life, though, maximize your insurance protection.

Insurance is, first and foremost, a tool to protect your family and replace your income if something should happen to you. Some people may think $1 million in life insurance sounds like a large amount. But if you think about never earning another dollar in your life and what that lost income would amount to, $1 million doesn't sound like so much anymore.

"Human life value" is a term used by life insurance companies to mean your total insurable value based on your earning history and potential.

However, we believe that human life value includes not just your financial potential, but also your character, health, knowledge, experiences, education, judgment, initiative, and ability to produce value for others. Your human life value creates all the physical things that you enjoy: your home, car, clothes, and furniture. All value results from the utilization of property or capacity by a human being. Any income you produce and the property you own come from your human life value.

Protect your human life value through maximization of coverage first. All other considerations come second.

You cannot be overinsured with life insurance. If you had a $10,000 car and insured it for $30,000, it would be overinsured; there would be too much incentive to crash the car. If you had a $1,000,0000 home and insured it for $1,500,000 million, it would create exposure for the insurance company. For some people, it would be an incentive to burn the house to the ground and make half a million dollars. Insurance companies that insure property will not overinsure you, and neither will life insurance companies.

The definition of insurance is the indemnification of a loss, or what would be lost if X occurred. Companies will assess the value of an asset and insure it for that amount or less (and no more). But it's hard to overestimate and easy to underestimate the value of your life.

Whatever amount of insurance a company will quote you, it will shortchange your actual value. Why? Because they base the number on a snapshot of where you are now. They won't factor in likely increases in income over your lifetime.

Insurance companies will usually only give you one times your net worth and ten times your annual income if you're near the end of your working life, or thirty times your annual income if you're young and have thirty or more years of work ahead of you. Again, don't think of life insurance as a lump sum, but as an income replacement.

When you know how much insurance to get—and *only* when you know that—then you choose what kind of insurance you want. If your current cash flow doesn't allow for optimally funded whole life right now, you can buy convertible term insurance in the meantime. Term is a great stopgap for a short period. If you buy term insurance, make sure that the company offers whole life, too, and that it will allow you to convert your policy regardless of your future health.

I sold insurance one-on-one from 1998–2006. During that time, I had a client who bought a ten-year term insurance policy. Just before he reached its end, he was diagnosed with a terminal illness. Thankfully, the term policy could be converted into a permanent policy before it expired, regardless of health.

Once you've got the right kind of insurance, your insurability is protected, no matter what. Of the over 2,000 life insurance carriers in the US, I know of maybe a dozen or so that I'd recommend for convertible term insurance.

If you have past health issues, you may be ineligible for insurance. Certain companies will give you a policy when you have some medical conditions, whereas others may not. Some are willing to insure certain types of risks. If you cannot get a policy on yourself, you can still open a policy on your spouse, child, parent, or business partners. I have whole life policies on my own life as well as on the lives of my spouse and kids.

OPTIMALLY FUND YOUR POLICY

One critical key of the Rockefeller Method is to fund your whole life policy or policies in the most advantageous way so you can use the living benefits of your policy as quickly as possible.

When we say to "optimally fund" your policy, what we mean is to add extra money to your policy than your premiums require. These additional premium dollars are called "paid-up additions." This money supports the growth of the policy so that your internal rate of return is accelerated in the early years of the policy instead of your having to wait ten or twelve years (or longer) to see a positive yield on your money. This not only increases your cash value more quickly—it also increases your death benefit.

If you put additional cash on top of your base premium, you can utilize that cash within thirty days of it going into your policy. You can also set up your policy so that at least 50%, in some cases as much as 90%, of the money you put into it in the first year shows up in the cash value.

There are limits on how much you can fund your policy, and if it is done incorrectly, it can negate the tax benefits. If you put too much money into your policy, it becomes a "modified endowment contract" (MEC). This means you are funding the policy at a level that exceeds the allowed funding amount or corridor of cash value to death benefit ratio based upon government rules. The government then treats it more like an annuity than an insurance contract.

This is easily avoided with simple calculations and communication. Be sure to talk with your Whole Life Certified specialist about how to properly fund your policy with paid-up additions.

Overall, the best method is to put as much into your policy as your cash flow will allow. Building to 15% of your income is ideal, but what is most important is getting started.

The great thing about paid-up additions is that you can stop them whenever you feel like it. When you reach retirement age, you may decide that you don't want to continue to pay more than the premiums into your policy. Then you can just pay the premium. Or you can use the cash value that you've stored up in your policy to pay the premium so you don't have to worry about more payments during the distribution phase of your financial life.

To properly structure and optimally fund a whole life policy, make sure you're working with the right agent. Agents get commissions on all forms of life insurance. Term life, universal life, and whole life insurance all have fairly similar commission percentages. At most companies, these range anywhere from 40–135% of first-year premiums, and then trail off as the years pass to 3–9%. I have heard of indexed universal life policies paying as much as 165% on base premiums.

Because whole life and universal life premiums are higher than term life premiums to start, the amount of money agents receive is higher even though the percentage is the same. Usually, commissions are paid to agents annually. If the policyholder doesn't pay for thirteen months or more, the commissions get pulled back from the agent. Agents can be incentivized to sell you a product that maximizes their commission. Some—not most—agents are unwilling to lower their commissions so that you can have more cash, so be careful.

A properly structured, optimally funded whole life policy can actually lower commissions by 50–80% because more of those optimally funded dollars are going to the cash value. Generally, life insurance companies hold onto the entire first year's base premium for ten years, using it for reserves to guarantee your death benefit. They also take the agent and underwriting costs into consideration. That's how they remain profitable and guarantee early death claims.

You can find a list of Whole Life Certified advisors at wholelifecertified.com.

CHOOSING THE RIGHT INSURANCE COMPANY

Once you have a Whole Life Certified specialist, the next step to setting up your properly structured, optimally funded whole life insurance is to pick a company with which to purchase your policy.

First, understand that there are two types: stock life insurance and mutual life insurance companies. As the name would imply, stock life insurance companies trade on the stock market, just like any other public company.

Mutual life insurance companies, on the other hand, do not trade on the stock market. There isn't a stock to buy or you can't own them in a fund inside of your whole life policy because they have no shares.

For good reason, a *participating* mutual insurance company is my preferred of the two. Stock life insurance companies, while they want their customers to be safe, also want to give their stockholders higher returns on their investments or split dividends between stockholders and policyholders.

In participating mutual life insurance companies, on the other hand, policyholders are owners, not stockholders. Profits are not split with any outside shareholders. While they still generate profits, stability and safety are the ultimate goals—and all the profits go to the owners, the policyholders.

Participating mutual life insurance companies are among the oldest companies in America. The average age of the top thirty-five life insurance companies in the country is over 100, the oldest being 184. Nineteen of the top thirty-five have been in business for over a century.

As these numbers would indicate, these companies are stable. Statistics drive the profits; as long as the equation is correct, these companies make predictable profits. A very small allocation of their accounts goes to the stock market, so their value isn't as volatile as the stock exchanges. And again, since there are no shareholders, Wall Street analysts and money managers cannot pressure these companies into making short-term, shortsighted decisions. Therefore, they are free to pursue long-term strategies and can be managed conservatively. They don't use margin and leverage, and they generate large amounts of cash that they pay out every year in large dividends.

Here are some other factors to consider when choosing your insurance company:

1. **A Ratings:** The company must have A ratings across the board, with Moody's, A.M. Best, Standard & Poor's, etc. Choose a top ten participating mutual insurance company.

2. **100+ Years Old:** Look for companies that have been around for at least a century.

3. **Solid Dividend History:** Make sure the company has paid dividends every year, including during world wars, recessions, depressions, etc.

4. **Loan Provisions:** Make sure that there is a fixed interest rate option.

5. **Convertible:** Make sure that the company's term insurance rates are competitive and convertible to whole life.

6. **High Early Cash Value:** Make sure that your policy can be designed to allow for a high cash value as quickly as possible.

7. **No Barriers for Paid Up Additions:** Make sure that there are minimal fees, expenses, or other obstacles standing in the way of easily optimally funding your policy.

There are about a dozen participating mutual life insurance companies that fulfill all of these requirements. You can find a list of them at wholelifecertified.com.

To effectively apply the Rockefeller Method and maximize its benefits, you must design your plan and structure your insurance properly. A poorly designed plan and policy will at best fail to deliver benefits, and at worst damage your long-term wealth. Be sure to work with a Whole Life Certified specialist who knows how to design the best plan for you.

CHAPTER 10

Find the Money to Fund Your Life and Legacy

Y ou may be thinking, *Whole life sounds great, but it's expensive. So where do I find the money to start my legacy, fund my policy, and build my fortune?*

We use a variety of methods and tools for freeing up cash to fund your Rockefeller plan. These include Mindful Cash Management, prioritizing your investing, using a variety of cash flow recovery strategies, and managing your plan with three or four specific accounts.

MINDFUL CASH MANAGEMENT

When you understand how your money is flowing, you can utilize Mindful Cash Management. This is very different from a budget. A budget is about cutting back, eliminating, and monitoring every single expenditure. It limits value creation and can be exhausting. On the other hand, without a budget or system, money can easily be wasted. Without automation for wealth capture, expenses often rise to meet or exceed one's income.

In Mindful Cash Management, the focus is on expansion over restriction, while being aware, accountable and creating automation, and wealth along the way. We are taught that expenses are negative. We are told to limit spending. But increasing the right expenses leads to more wealth and profit. Not all expenses are created equal.

Expenses fall into four main categories:

1. **Destructive Expenses:** These expenses involve borrowing to consume or overdraft fees, or any other draw on your funds that negatively affects your life by creating poverty rather than prosperity. When you spend more than you have and borrow to consume, the loan and interest become a destructive expense.

2. **Lifestyle Expenses:** These expenses, such as utilities, clothing, and food, support the essentials in life. They also include vacations and things that are fun and create memories but don't build tangible assets. I recommend using cash for these expenses. Rather than cut these expenses out, manage them wisely. **Never borrow to consume.** People are taught to wait until retirement to finally enjoy their hard-earned money, and then, in retirement, they finally have permission to enjoy life. That is the path to becoming a miserable millionaire. A broke millionaire has money but never enjoys life or the money they earn. If you never spend any money, why have it in the first place? Expenses can support your life and lifestyle expenses support you in feeling fulfilled. There is nothing wrong with these expenses—as long as they are managed properly.

   NOTE: You may finance a car or home, which are most likely lifestyle expenses (unless you Airbnb or Turo those assets) as they do not provide cash flow. Be cautious about how much you spend and borrow, and ensure that you are automatically saving money off the top of your earnings first and building your peace of mind fund/liquidity.

3. **Protective Expenses:** These expenses transfer risk. They protect your property and human life value, including your mindset and happiness. This is the area that often gets overlooked. Protective expenses include your liquid savings and a minimum of six months' expenses which, with cash value over time, will be years. Even though savings won't be overly productive in terms of earning interest, they will be there to support you and prevent you from worrying about money. Protective expenses include your will, trust, and asset protection. Other protective expenses include life insurance, disability insurance, medical insurance, auto insurance, and emergency preparedness.

4. **Productive Expenses:** These are expenses that allow you to expand your cash flow, grow your business, and build assets. They might be investments in your business, like hiring a great employee. Or they might be related to developing skillsets, whereby whole new worlds of opportunities are opened up for you. If you put a dollar into a productive expense, more than a dollar comes out the other side. Any investment that is an asset that creates cash flow and appreciates can be classified as a productive expense. These are expenses that enhance your life both now and in the future, whereas others are of the moment, like lifestyle expenses, or contribute to poverty, like destructive expenses. Productive expenses build profit and prosperity.

The goal of Mindful Cash Management is to *eliminate* destructive expenses, *manage* lifestyle expenses, *address* protective expenses, and *increase* productive expenses.

PRIORITIZE YOUR INVESTING

When managing your finances, make sure that you invest in yourself. Make more money by investing in the most critical skill sets that allow you to add maximum value. Keep more of what you make. Then grow your money.

Before you start accumulating money in retirement plans, make sure that you have built your financial foundation and plugged your financial leaks. Focus on creating a state of economic independence where your assets create enough cash flow to cover your expenses before locking your money away or speculating with it. When you are economically independent and have fully funded your whole life insurance from year to year, you will have the funds and the freedom to capitalize on opportunities that may take longer to produce cash flow. Once you have your foundation in place, you may be able to handle some speculation in an investment with a future upside, but no immediate cash flow.

People often speculate on the path to economic independence and experience some false starts. It is easy to spend money after an investment pays off when there is a lack of infrastructure. Most financial models emphasize the accumulation of money in plans that provide limited to no cash flow (and limit access to those funds when cash flow opportunities arise). Getting your financial house in order begins with guarding against uncertainty. This includes having your peace of mind fund (six months of liquid savings), your life insurance cash value (three of the six months' aforementioned savings can be inside the policy), and money for emergency preparedness.

Without this foundation, all of your investments are at risk with any financial surprise or issue. We can all expect financial surprises, but we can mitigate risk so those surprises don't necessarily derail us. Make sure to build liquidity, transfer risk, and plug financial leaks before moving on to anything else. This will help you avoid the risk of losing momentum and everything you have worked so hard for.

Do not leave all of your efforts exposed. Secure your foundation. Protect your money in such a way that it can't be confiscated or lost through unexpected circumstances by creating a more sustainable plan, like the Rockefellers did.

Once your foundation is set, the next focus is on creating cash flow to reach economic independence. Each person's plan is unique. To maximize returns and minimize risk, know your Investor DNA. Once you discover your Investor DNA, you become a better investor. Rather than diversifying by investing in things outside of your expertise, it is key to focus on the best asset or investment that can support you in creating cash flow.

Diversification is a great strategy when you have already built wealth and want to preserve that wealth. To grow your wealth, it is key to create cash flow and take an active role in the process of finding investments in areas you are driven to learn about and that utilize your competencies.

USE CASH FLOW RECOVERY STRATEGIES

Even if you don't have great cash flow right now, the Rockefeller Method helps you find extra money and hold onto it. Right now, some of your money is being lost to financial institutions, taxes, loans, and inefficiencies. If you can reclaim that money using what I call "cash flow optimization" or "cash recovery," that money can go into an optimally funded whole life policy that protects and grows your wealth rather than losing it.

The goal is to keep more of what you make and boost your bottom line by focusing on the "4 I's of Efficiency":

If you get a tax refund every year, you are overpaying taxes. In other words, you are giving the government an interest-free loan over the year. If you increase your exemptions and decrease your tax overpayment, you can use that extra cash to start building your family trust. Instead of reinvesting the interest you earn on your investments, you can put it into your optimally funded whole life policy. In the policy, that money can grow tax-free.

Paying off or restructuring inefficient loans is a great way to free up cash flow that you can then put into your optimally funded whole life. People often think that what matters most is paying off loans as quickly as possible. Suze Orman is always saying it's important to shorten your mortgage and other loans. However, if you shorten your mortgage or loans, it forces you into higher payments, which can create more risk and increase your debt-to-income ratio, lowering your cash flow and ability to borrow.

Your debt-to-income ratio is the percentage of every dollar you make that is required to go toward a loan payment, whether principal or interest. You can use the Cash Flow Index we discuss below to determine which loan is the biggest cash hog and free up your debt-to-income fastest. Paying off inefficient loans, especially revolving loans like credit cards, may even help your credit score, which could help lower your interest on other loans.

Take a look at your investment portfolio to see what your earnings are. What is the interest rate on your savings, money markets, or CDs? What are you earning on your mutual fund or stocks you may have?

If you could cash out a CD that is not performing very well, you could use that money to pay off an 8% interest rate loan that's costing you $800 a month in payment. That immediately increases cash flow, which could allow you to renegotiate interest rates on other loans as well, thereby freeing up even more cash flow beyond the $800 per month. Take this freed-up cash and capitalize your optimally funded whole life.

You can even consider extending loans when interest rates are low. Then you can fund your policy for more long-term wealth—more money in your pocket as well as added stability and options for you along the way. You can refinance your fifteen-year mortgage to a thirty-year mortgage and divert your higher mortgage payments into an optimally funded whole life policy.

From 2021 and a decade or more before, this was a strategy with lower interest rates that could be used to your advantage from a cash standpoint. You would have had enough money in the policy fifteen years later to pay off the remainder of the mortgage. Then you could have taken what was going towards the mortgage to put money back into the policy.

You may consider wrapping low cash flow index loans (see below) into your mortgage, thereby making the interest potentially tax deductible while lowering the payment and interest rate. Like credit card interest, the interest on many loans is not tax-deductible. Mortgage interest can be tax-deductible in the US, depending on your income. If you consolidate those other loans into your mortgage, you can gain tax advantages while improving your cash flow. It is important to note that if you have a history of spending more than you make, or increasing your consumer loans year-by-year, wrapping loans into your mortgage can be dangerous. If you merely spend the additional savings or worse, use the additional cash flow to pay for new loans on depreciating assets. You will chip away at your legacy.

It's not just restructuring mortgages that can help free up cash flow. Suppose you have a vehicle that's been paid off. You may be able to refinance it at a preferred interest rate to pay off higher interest rate credit cards. The money you save can then be put into your optimally funded whole life. A car loan—an installment loan—is a better for your credit than a revolving loan like a credit card because the revolving loan is ongoing while an installment loan is finite.

If you can restructure your inefficient loans so you have the lowest payments required with the best interest rates and tax advantages, you free up money which can then go into your optimally funded whole life. It's not costing you anything extra; it's just using the flow of your money more efficiently.

IMPROVE CASH FLOW WITH THE CASH FLOW INDEX

The cash flow index (CFI) is a system for identifying the most effective way to pay off your inefficient loans and free up cash flow.

You can find the CFI of any loan by taking the balance of your loan and dividing it by the minimum payment. If your index is a low number, then the loan is inefficient—a cash hog that requires a high payment relative to the balance. A higher number, on the other hand, indicates a more efficient loan.

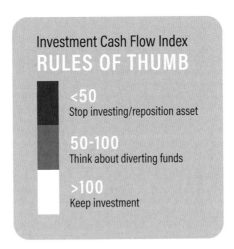

As you can see on the chart, any loan with a CFI between zero and fifty is in the danger zone and you may look to restructure or eliminate it as quickly as possible. Any loan with a CFI greater than 100 is in the freedom zone and not a priority to pay off, from a cash flow standpoint.

To make this more concrete, let's consider a few different loans:

LOAN	BALANCE	INTEREST RATE	MONTHLY PAYMENT	CASH FLOW INDEX
Mortgage	$248,000	6.5%	$1,750	141 ($248,000 ÷ $1,750)
Auto	$18,000	5%	$450	40 ($18,000 ÷ $450)
Credit Card 1	$6,000	15%	$125	48 ($6,000 ÷ $125)
Credit Card 2	$14,000	12%	$300	46 ($14,000 ÷ $300)

Using the CFI, this is the order in which we would recommend these loans get paid off:

Most people would advocate paying off Credit Card 1 first, since it has the highest interest rate and the lowest balance. It does make sense to pay it off quickly and then use the additional $125 per month you've freed up to pay down the other loans.

But the CFI reveals the fastest and safest way to repay all of these loans. It frees up the most cash the soonest, which can then be rolled into paying down subsequent loans. Pay the extra money toward an inefficient loan with a low index. Paying off a loan with a low index has the potential to free up much more money. This could mean building savings faster, creating more liquidity, providing more peace of mind, reducing forced payments, and even improving credit scores, which could improve interest rates on other loans.

You may even initially delay paying anything extra to loans. Instead, you could put the money into your optimally funded whole life insurance system and then pay the loan off in full when there is enough cash in your plan. Depending on the interest rate, this may save you money and create more wealth in the future as you build up liquidity, earn interest, and gain the benefits of whole life insurance.

When you are restructuring loans, look at refinancing to a lower interest rate or a longer amortization term so that the loan will be more cash-flow efficient. You can also manage and restructure your loans so that your loan interest is tax deductible, as with many mortgages. If you restructure a fifteen-year mortgage into a thirty-year fixed-rate mortgage, you can improve your cash flow because the payment is lower today *and* paying interest for a longer period could amount to hundreds of thousands of dollars in tax savings over time. On one hand, you get tax deductions on interest, and on the other hand, your earnings are tax-preferred inside of an optimally funded whole life policy.

This depends on the interest rate you pay versus the dividends you earn, so make sure to meet with a Whole Life Certified agent to address your unique circumstance. You can even take a cash value loan against the policy and pay off your home in fifteen years, if that is your objective.

USE THREE (OR FOUR) ACCOUNTS IN YOUR FINANCIAL HOUSE

Getting your financial house in order also means creating the proper account structure. Ideally, you want to set up three types of accounts.

1. **Peace of Mind Account:** This account is dedicated to providing you with staying power in times of limited cash flow. It reduces risk and creates additional liquidity, enabling you to handle the unexpected. It is essential that this account be completely separate from your checking account. This could be a savings or even a money market account. The target is to have a minimum of six months' worth of expenses in reserve. I recommend having two or three of those six months in a savings/peace of mind account, one month in cash or precious metals in a safe, and up to three months in your properly structured, optimally funded whole life insurance policy. Having money in precious metals or a safe protects you in case of bank failures, identity theft, or even an IRS lien so you can still have access to money to take care of your family until you can access your accounts.

2. **Wealth Creation Account:** This account is focused on growing cash flow and improving the efficiency of your loans. Properly structured, optimally funded whole life is the best structure for a Wealth Creation Account. Premiums for your whole life policy can be deducted directly from your Peace of Mind account. Your Wealth Creation Account can be used for productive expenses like making investments or simply for storing your cash.

3. **Living Wealthy Account:** You are your best asset, and this account facilitates and creates structure around your enjoyment of life. It is for lifestyle expenses. If 15% of your personal income goes to your Wealth Creation Account, take an additional 3% (or more) and put

it in this account to boost your quality of life. This account is for value-based spending. What do you value? The list might include things that other people consider wasteful or indulgent, but if you are saving 15% in your Wealth Capture Account, what you spend it on doesn't matter (as long as it isn't destructive expenses). This is for you and your best life. Putting money in this account is an essential reminder and affirmation that you are doing the right things for your finances and deserve to celebrate.

4. Finally, there is a bonus account: a Charitable Giving Account. This account allows you to set aside money for charities, organizations, and causes you believe in and support groups and activities that matter to you. Focusing on getting your financial house in order and acquiring a properly structured, optimally funded whole life policy will give you the power to be more charitable throughout your lifetime.

GET RICH THE RIGHT WAY

There's a law in finance called Parkinson's Law, which states that in the absence of a financial plan, an increase in income will be met with an increase in expense. By setting up the proper account structure, you can capture your wealth instead of having it sucked up by living expenses. You are your greatest asset. Protect yourself and your mindset.

Your strong financial foundation will bring forth peace of mind, allowing you to become more productive. Properly structured, optimally funded whole life is NOT a get-rich-quick scheme. This is about sustainable wealth—getting rich the right way and staying that way. Whole life provides a safe, steady, and consistent way to grow your wealth. With that stable financial foundation, you create more staying power with more savings. With economic independence, you can swing for the fences in your unique areas of knowledge and interest.

Financially successful people can capitalize on opportunities. Utilizing your whole life allows you to do this—as opposed to watching opportunities pass you by because you didn't have the financial means to capitalize on or implement them.

Regardless of your income, your goals for the future, or your current cash flow restraints, if your optimally funded whole life is set up properly and your financial foundation is well designed, you can create a legacy, initiate a new path forward, and change your family's financial future.

For some, it may begin with securing a convertible term insurance policy. This locks in your insurability and gives you the ability to convert the policy to whole life when you have better cash flow. Whether you put in $100 or $10,000 a month, a system can be designed to work for you. Even if you are living paycheck to paycheck, optimally funded whole life can work for you as long as you have some income. Even if you have a medical issue that makes you ineligible for life insurance, you can set up a policy on someone with whom you have an insurable interest: a child, sibling, spouse, or even a business partner.

A properly structured, optimally funded whole life insurance policy is perfect for you if you are married or plan on getting married, if you have children or plan on having children, or if you are starting a business or plan on starting a business. It can help you pay for your kids' college, pay off loans, or finance your home or car. You can use it as a cash reserve for investing, as seed capital, or as part of your Peace of Mind Fund. You can use it for short-term and long-term money management decisions.

Whole life can be the driver that perpetuates your legacy via your trust and an alternative to the banking system your family can use to capture interest for generations to come—interest that would otherwise have been lost to financial institutions. That's why optimally funded whole life is the heart of the Rockefeller Method.

CHAPTER 11

Maximize Your Financial Efficiency and Earning Potential

S aving money is great. What most people don't realize is how much saving can be accelerated by plugging leaks and setting up a new system to eliminate bank loans.

Do you know where your money is going, how it flows through your hands, and where it ends up? When it comes to recapturing your wealth, what do you think is more important: Paying off loans? Reducing expenses? Earning a higher rate of return?

Todd Langford of Truth Concepts has produced an amazing calculator of your "maximum potential." When you calculate your maximum potential, it becomes easy to see the benefits of saving money (without painful budgeting) and recovering cash rather than seeking a higher rate of return.

Your full earning potential is reduced over time by eroding factors such as taxes, debt service, inflation, and lifestyle expenses. If you can save $5,000 a year in tax, another $5,000 in interest, and another $5,000 on hidden fees (like admin fees, legal fees, 12B-1 fees, or commissions) or even poor insurance design that leads to duplicate coverage, increasing your costs, that's $15,000.

Do you know how much money you would have to invest to find $15,000 a year in cash flow? If your investment earned 5%, you'd have to have $300,000 invested. But you can get the same return simply by optimizing cash flow and recapturing costs.

Let's look at an analysis over a thirty-year period. To make it easy, for this example, let's say you have no assets, no 401(k), and no money set aside. What you have is your greatest asset: your earning power and potential. Suppose your income is $100,000 per year. That means that over the next thirty years, a total of $3 million will flow through your hands. This is assuming that you have no increase in income and no earnings on that investment.

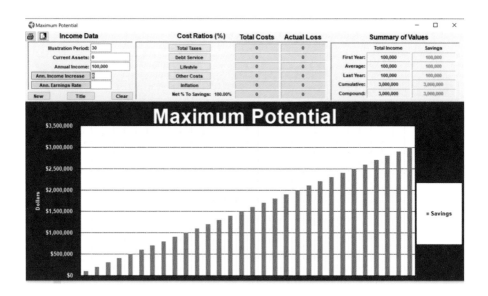

We know that you can increase your earnings over time, so let's add 5% a year. If we calculate the additional 5% over the next thirty years, your $3 million becomes $6.6 million a year you can put into your cash flow.

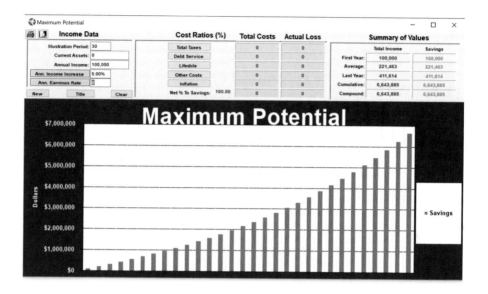

| Maximum Potential | | | | | | | | — □ ✕ |

Income Data			Cost Ratios (%)	Total Costs	Actual Loss		Summary of Values	
Illustration Period:	30		Total Taxes	0	0		Total Income	Savings
Current Assets:	0		Debt Service	0	0	First Year:	100,000	100,000
Annual Income:	100,000		Lifestyle	0	0	Average:	221,463	221,463
Ann. Income Increase	5.00%		Other Costs	0	0	Last Year:	411,614	411,614
Ann. Earnings Rate	0		Inflation	0	0	Cumulative:	6,643,885	6,643,885
New	Title	Clear	Net % To Savings: 100.00	0	0	Compound:	6,643,885	6,643,885

There's one more assumption at work so far: that you're basically keeping your money under the mattress and it's not working or earning for you at all. So now let's assume that you've learned some optimally funded whole life insurance principles and can make a better return on your money than you would by stashing it under the mattress.

Let's assume that you're earning 5% interest on your money. Now your total income over thirty years increases to a whopping $12.9 million. That $12.9 million is your earning potential. That is how much money will pass through your hands over thirty years, given the variables above.

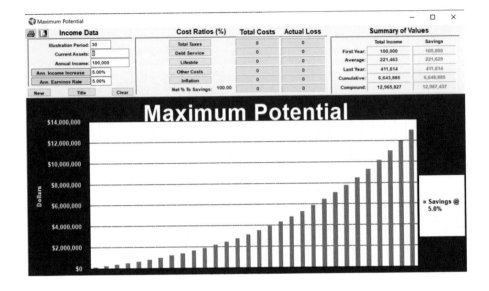

THREE MAIN ERODERS OF INCOME

The question is, how much of that money are you holding onto, and how much just slips away?

Many factors can erode your income over thirty years. We'll focus on the three most powerful eroding factors: taxes, loan interest, and lifestyle.

Taxes

You know what's funny about taxes? *Nothing.* Taxes suck. They have a huge impact on how much money you hold onto. This includes not only income tax, but at least a dozen other taxes as well. Think about the cumulative effect of state or provincial income tax, property tax, sales tax, estate tax, self-employment tax, luxury tax, and on and on. You have to pay taxes to work, live, drive, eat, buy, sell—hell, even to die. (That is, if you don't use the Rockefeller Method and plan properly.)

A conservative estimate puts the amount of income that goes to taxes each year at .40 cents of every dollar. When we calculate 40% of your income going to taxes over a thirty-year period, that $12.9 million suddenly drops to $7.8 million. That's just after paying taxes, nothing else.

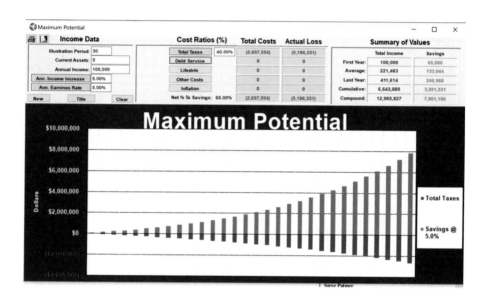

Loan Interest

The second major factor is the loans we have and the interest we pay on them. This includes mortgages, car loans, credit cards, student loans, and business loans.

Any money that goes toward loan interest is money leaving your pocket. Americans put an estimated average of 35% of their income toward loans. When we factor that in over thirty years, the $7.8 million becomes $2.9 million.

We've already dropped your earning potential by $9.7 million just by paying taxes and loans. We haven't even factored in the cost of lifestyle, the money you spend living your life.

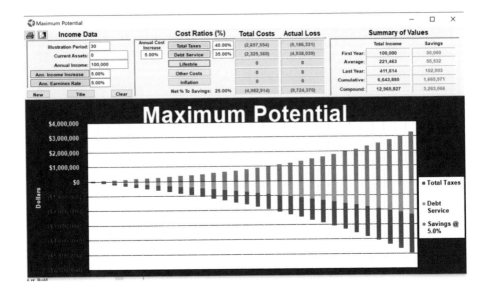

Lifestyle Expenses

Lifestyle cost for Americans averages 23.5% of income. When we factor that in over thirty years, the amount of money we have left over sinks to $216,097.

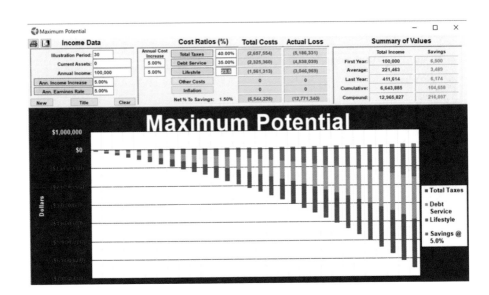

Pretty shocking, isn't it? How is someone used to a $100,000 annual income going to survive on a total of less than $200,000 in savings if they stop working? How can you keep more of the money you make without cutting back?

Most fee-based planners will tell you that the solution is to focus on increasing your rate of return. High risk equals high return, they say. However, this can be a very risky proposition considering that risk means a higher chance of losing. There is this idea of taking more risk and tolerating more volatility (lowering certainty along the way).

Let's follow their advice and see how the numbers play out. To make a point in this example, we'll use some magic product that increases your rate of return. (We all know that there is no magic product; this is for the purpose of illustration.) Instead of 5% interest on your earnings, let's increase it to 10%. This increases our total amount left over to $607,700 from $216,097. This is certainly still insufficient for twenty or thirty years of retirement and will not replace the income this person earned during their lifetime.

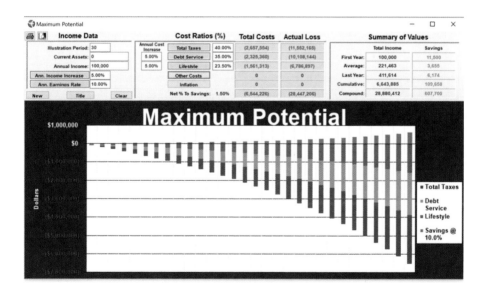

Increasing your rate of return from 5% to 10% generally indicates volatility. And what if, right before you were to retire, the market dropped 10%, 20%, or even 30%? Risk puts your life savings and legacy in jeopardy!

Simply increasing your rate of return is not the solution. However, it is what is taught by most typical financial planners with the "high risk equals high rate of return" and "low risk equals low rate of return" mindset. Sad, if you ask me.

KEEP MORE MONEY IN YOUR POCKET

What's the solution to keeping more money in your pocket? Minimizing those eroding factors.

First of all, we want to focus more on reducing your taxes and loan interest and less on reducing your lifestyle expenses. We want you to be able to keep your lifestyle and enhance it over time.

Let's isolate taxes and loans and go back to the 5% earnings rate, which brings your total after thirty years to $216,097. Using cash value insurance and some basic tax strategy, you can decrease your tax burden by 10%, meaning 10% of the 40% average, so 4% total. Now you are paying a total of 36% on taxes.

You can reduce those expenses by another half when you use the Cash Flow Index to identify inefficient loans and pay them off with your cash value. But to be conservative, we'll say you have to reduce your loan payments from 35% to 20%. Rather than paying interest, you can use your cash value. Between saving tax on your cash value, capturing dollars otherwise paid to term insurance, as well as renegotiating interest rates, restructuring loans, and paying off higher interest rate loans with lower interest rate earnings, the 15 percent reduction is conservative.

Using your cash value rather than a bank to finance things makes a big difference. Now you've gone from holding onto just $216,097 of your $12.9 million to keeping just under $2.7 million. That's a pretty dramatic difference.

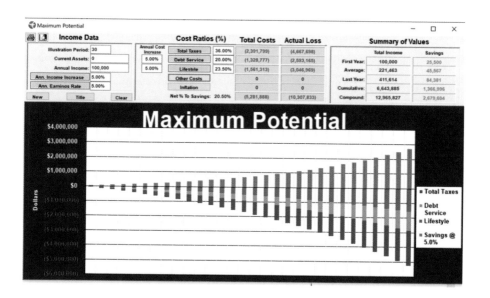

It's important to note that this was all done at no additional risk to you. You obviously never want to neglect your rate of return. But you should also focus on keeping more of what you make through efficiency and maximizing your earning potential. Efficiency gives you the greatest impact with the least risk.

Chasing a higher rate of return by exposing your money and legacy is not the answer. The answer is to focus on leverage, efficiency, utilization of your money, and decreasing eroding factors. Utilizing whole life insurance, you can minimize your taxes, lower your interest costs, and invest in yourself.

The key is to take the money you free up using these techniques to fund your optimally funded whole life, invest in a skill set, and improve your lifestyle.

The list of benefits includes having more cash and more access to that cash, keeping your money earning while you borrow, protecting your money from bad economies and financial predators, recovering the cost of term insurance, and limiting your tax exposure. You can mitigate and manage your risk while capitalizing on all of your income and maximizing your potential by keeping more of what you make along the way.

CHAPTER 12

Build Your Team to Protect Your Legacy

N ow that we've covered the details and nuances, benefits and comparisons of insurance, it is time to design your trust and optimally funded whole life insurance the Rockefeller way.

The Rockefellers use a network of trusts and a Family Office to keep their fortune alive. Their Family Office is a comprehensive, coordinated team of financial professionals that includes, among others:

- Attorneys
- Bankers
- Investment Advisors
- Real Estate Investors
- Risk Managers
- Insurance Planners

Rockefeller-style Family Offices are cost-prohibitive, which is why most people don't use them—and many people don't even know that such things exist. Having a team of financial professionals working for your family alone would require hundreds of millions of dollars to justify the expense. But thankfully there are fractional, or virtual Family Offices that can support you even if you are just starting out.

If you don't have an integrated team that stays in close communication, critical financial components will slip through the cracks. And when your finances are mishandled properly, it robs you of wealth and time. Fragmented advice can also end up working against you.

For example, if your accountant disagrees with your attorney, it's a problem. Or worse, if you don't have someone on your team handling an important area of your finances, you remain exposed, jeopardizing your legacy and risking your dreams. What happens if you have a real estate investor who disagrees with your fee-based advisor? Hell, insurance people don't even agree on the type or amount of insurance you should have; how would they possibly agree with your investment management style?

I experienced this in my own life when my first attorney and first accountant disagreed and did not communicate. This miscommunication and lack of coordination eventually led to my shutting down one LLC and starting an S Corp, not to mention seven years of dealing with extra paperwork and explanations to the IRS.

When you don't have a comprehensive team, finances feel more complex and are more likely to be incomplete. When salespeople handle aspects of your finances, expect unnecessary exposure or a lack of coordination that confiscates your wealth and creates risk.

I learned about Family Offices in my early twenties, when I sat in a boardroom filled with experts in every area of finance. This team analyzed the tax implications, risks, and ownership of an investment while communicating and doing actual due diligence, and the client wasn't even in the room.

This is exactly what you would hope a fiduciary would be, while so many still end up peddling mutual funds for fees.

BUILDING YOUR TEAM

Inherited money doesn't change a person's relationship with money—it enhances that relationship. A spender who inherits money will spend it. A saver will save it. An investor will invest it, and so on.

You want to implement the Rockefeller Method and leave behind generational wealth for your family. But how do you protect the wealth from heirs who aren't ready to manage so much money? How do you make sure your descendants experience wealth and opportunity, but not the opportunity to throw Great Gatsby parties in waterfront mansions like spoiled brats?

The Rockefellers designed trusts to protect their family's wealth. But a trust is a trust because you give up legal ownership of assets and entrust them to someone else. Is it still possible, then, to maintain some control over the family wealth and make sure it is preserved?

Ownership is a key aspect to consider with life insurance. How you own your whole life policy and set up the beneficiary have major implications with regard to estate tax (among other things). Most policies are owned individually, yet it may make more sense for them to be owned by an LLC or a trust, like an asset protection trust.

There are pros and cons to each type of ownership. It is essential that you meet with appropriate legal counsel to make sure the considerations are specific to your planning. The key is to start somewhere. Don't get lost in all the details. Begin by setting up a separate account at your bank for wealth capture. Automate your savings by paying yourself first. Find areas where you're losing and leaking money. Apply for insurance to see what you can get.

Delaying setting up your life insurance could actually be a big mistake. Look at you Aussies out there. Australia's government changed the rules for new policyholders, eliminating tax benefits and changing the design of insurance policies. Personally, I have a family history of kidney issues, so maybe you're in better health now than you're going to be later. Waiting could be the difference between the best health rating to being denied.

Plan for the best, but prepare for the worst. This philosophy is not about sacrificing or just saving, delaying or deferring—it's about building a lasting legacy. It's about creating alternatives to the bank so you can take advantage of opportunities as they arise. It's about freeing up cash flow without infringing upon your lifestyle. It's about being able to plan and work toward your future vision while living well.

THE CEO AND BOARD OF TRUSTEES FOR YOUR TRUST

In order to create a more personalized trust that represents you and your family's values, it is critical to have a Family Constitution. This is especially true if you have substantial asset value or whole life insurance and leave behind a sizeable sum of money. A Family Constitution and board of trustees will be critical for the protection of the family fortune after you are gone.

First, a board of trustees can be established to help manage the family wealth if you're not around to do so. A board of trustees is a great way to make sure your family turns out like the Rockefellers and not the Vanderbilts.

Today, I am the figurative CEO of my trust. It's not an actual position and you won't find me identified as "chief executive officer" in my trust documents. But during my lifetime, I will continue to fulfill the responsibilities of a traditional CEO for my trust.

A CEO typically has three key responsibilities: establishing the company vision, establishing the company culture, and looking after the shareholders' financial interests. And that's exactly what I do for my family's trust. I've established the vision by writing it down in detail in my Family Constitution as a preamble to our family trust. I've established the culture by setting an example for my kids, who will one day do the same for their kids. We also have semi-regular family meetings and have collaborated to create our family mission and family guidance (set of rules).

While I am alive, I'm the one adding money to the trust and guiding it for the benefit of my heirs. My trust also states that I have the power to overrule any withdrawal from the trust during my lifetime. So, while the trustees have the legal right to distribute assets from the trust at any time, they can't do it without my approval.

At some point, however, I won't be around to personally protect the family trust. What then? Again, let's look to the example of a corporation, which may have a board of trustees who are bound by company bylaws. These bylaws may give direction on selling the company, what to do in case of a hostile takeover, or how to handle misbehavior from someone within the company, for example. If the bylaws don't spell out exactly what to do, the board can vote on what action to take.

Well, your trust can have a board of trustees, too. And if you choose your board carefully and give them specific instructions when it's appropriate, your board of trustees can protect the family wealth for you after you're gone. They can vote on when to approve distributions to heirs, when to sell assets or businesses, and how to handle lawsuits against the family. They can even decide to stop giving distributions to an heir with an alcohol or other problem that would make access to more money destructive.

CHOOSING A BOARD OF TRUSTEES AND A TRUST PROTECTOR

Clearly, selecting the people who will protect your family's wealth after you're gone is not a matter to be taken lightly. You must seek out those who best understand your financial philosophy, will respect your wishes, and will best represent the choices you'd make if you were still around to make them. You'll find an exercise in the Legacy Builder course that will help you choose your board. Get it for free at rockefellersbook.com/legacy.

My advice is to start with people who share your values and can teach those values to the next generation. Another way to think about it is, if you were to start a company today, who would you partner with or put on the board of directors?

You can choose to have three or five members, as long as it is an odd number. Here is some language from my trust documents for reference:

> **Appointment of Initial Trustee:** I appoint a Board of Trustees collectively acting together as if they are the Trustees described within this Trust. Unless otherwise indicated, the Board shall make decisions by a majority vote in number. Moe Abdou shall act as the Chairman of the Board of Trustees.

I chose my board by considering what each member represents that is similar to a characteristic or value in me. That way, they can teach my kids or grandkids if I'm not around to do so. Some of the skills, values, and characteristics I considered were Soul Purpose, business acumen, and emotional and financial IQ. I gave a lot of thought to who best understood the financial philosophies I espouse. It is important that they invest time with my kids and family and that my wife Carrie can lean on them for help with our finances as well.

I chose Moe Abdou to be the chairman of our board of trustees because I believe his personal qualities fit the job requirements in an extraordinary way. When I pass away, Moe's responsibilities as chairman will include calling the board together when there's an issue that requires action, making sure appropriate decorum is observed during meetings, guiding decisions in a way that matches the Family Constitution philosophy, and making sure all decisions by the board are enacted.

But what if my board of trustees, despite all the evidence that they will follow my wishes, decides to go rogue and start investing the family wealth in some wild scheme I would never have approved? Of course, I am confident that this will never happen. But in case the board votes to do something that would put my trust in jeopardy, I've appointed my attorney as my trust protector. My attorney is not a trustee and doesn't vote on how to manage the trust, but he can overrule the board whenever he believes they're not acting in the best interest of the trust. He can also remove and replace trustees who no longer seem to be acting upon my wishes for the trust.

Because I have assembled a carefully chosen board of trustees and appointed a trust protector, all of whom know me and my philosophy well, I can feel more confident that my family trust will be managed responsibly even after I'm gone. Through the years, the members of my board of trustees or the trust protector may change, but the philosophy and principles will not. The legacy I leave for my family will be more likely to carry on.

Other wealthy families, such as the Phipps family, have utilized the same method employed by the Rockefellers. Henry Phipps grew up in the same neighborhood in Pittsburgh as Andrew Carnegie and was known around town for being a shrewd financier, so when Andrew started the Carnegie Steel Company, he made Henry Phipps a business partner. This made Phipps a very wealthy man, as he was the second largest shareholder in Carnegie Steel, one of the richest companies in American history.

A believer in philanthropy like the Rockefellers, Phipps gave much of his wealth away and also believed in leaving a lasting legacy for his five children and their descendants. That's why he founded the Bessemer Trust in 1907.

The Bessemer Trust was created to be the Family Office for the Phipps family. Its purpose was to manage the family finances in order for wealth to last for generations. By all accounts and six generations later, the Bessemer Trust has succeeded. In fact, Henry Phipps's great-grandson, Stuart S. Janney III, is the current chairman of the board of directors for the trust. A letter from Henry Phipps to his son, Henry Carnegie Phipps, written shortly after the trust's founding, has been immortalized for its wisdom and foresight. Here is the letter, reprinted in its entirety:

Henry Phipps
87th Street & Fifth Avenue
New York

June 16, 1911

My dear Hal,

I have today transferred to your name two million dollars $2,000,000 in bonds and two million dollars $2,000,000 in stock of the Bessemer Investment Company which I wish you to regard as a trust from me for the benefit of yourself and your children after you. It is my desire that neither the stock nor the bonds of the Company shall pass out of my family and that you will agree among yourselves that the others shall have an opportunity to buy at a fair price the stock and bonds of any one before a different disposition can be made. I hope that the management of the affairs of the Company shall meet with approval of each one but should a difference of opinion arise I desire that the judgment of a majority of you shall be controlling on all questions of policy. I advise that you approve action by the Board of Directors of the Company in reserving all net profits as additions to surplus account and in declaring no dividend on the stock for at least ten (10) years. I urge upon you to live within your income and not to be a borrower on your own account or through the Company.

Realizing that changed conditions may arise which will require freedom in action to meet them I have not fixed rigid limitations as to possession and control of this property but have indicated my earnest desire that a prudent and conservative management of the Company shall be maintained and enforced and that each of you shall put proper restrictions upon your expenditures and lay aside a reasonable proportion of your income.

I have full confidence that this advice will be respected and followed by all of my children.

Your affectionate father,
Henry Phipps

One slice of insight is Phipps's choice not to include "fixed rigid limitations" on the family assets. While the Vanderbilt story shows that giving free rein to family members and allowing them to spend a fortune can be disastrous, there is wisdom in not making the rules too rigid.

My attorney shared with me a story of a family trust that left money for education, but because the family didn't foresee the changes that would take place in education, like the cost of computers, software, fees, or travel, the rigid rules meant some expenses couldn't be paid for.

It's impossible to write specific rules for a future you do not know.

There is some wisdom in trusting your heirs to make good choices using the intellectual legacy you've also left behind. As with so many things, harmony, adaptability, and a common philosophy are key.

CHAPTER 13

Create Your Lasting Legacy with a Family Constitution

What do you want your legacy to be? It's how you live, not just what you leave. It's about passing on more than just money from generation to generation; it's passing on values, philosophies, contributions, and opportunity. Wealthy families treat legacy like a business.

This is done through proper setup and execution of a trust, your board of trustees, and a Family Constitution. My Family Constitution takes up thirty-eight pages of my seventy-plus-page trust document.

Yes, I was wordier than my attorney. But I know that I'm leaving behind more than just money. I'm also leaving behind an intellectual legacy of wisdom, knowledge, and values.

Below are excerpts from my Family Constitution. My method is to write down a premise, a vision, a purpose, and a strategy for each area of my life where I have wisdom to share. I learned this from John and Missy Butcher and their phenomenal Lifebook program.

1. The *premise* is my view of the world as I know it.

2. The *vision* is the way I see myself and my family having an impact on the world.

3. The *purpose* is the reason why the vision is important.

4. The *strategy* is how to implement the vision. (Strategy is the least important of these factors initially because it could change over time.)

Below, I share excerpts from the financial section of my Family Constitution so you can glean some knowledge from them and maybe even get inspired. Feel free to borrow, steal, or modify any or all of it as you see fit—whatever resonates with you and your family.

PREMISE

Money is a man-made tool of efficient exchange. It's a by-product of value creation. Although money may be finite, the number of times it can change hands, be utilized, and facilitate exchange is infinite.

To have money, it's essential to be a wise steward and accountable to being productive with money. Cash flow is superior to net worth.

It's not only possible to have a lot of money and be spiritual; wealth and spirituality go hand in hand.

No one individual is an expert in everything when it comes to finance. No one cares more about your money than you, so be a steward of your money.

No amount of luck, discipline, rate of return, or savings will ever matter if you can't overcome the scarcity mentality, which will inevitably destroy wealth.

Abundance can exist because even if the amount of money is finite, it can change hands an infinite number of times through exchange. And we build wealth when that exchange solves problems, creates value, and serves others through our Soul Purpose. Prosperity is the evidence of value creation.

Personal legacy begins today and during one's lifetime. When money and Soul Purpose are aligned, legacy is lived.

There's a richness of experience in building knowledge that will be used to serve others and ultimately increase daily production. Building one's Soul Purpose is key to building one's net worth. Soul Purpose is, in fact, the only true financial security that exists.

VISION

I envision a world where Soul Purpose is the number one priority for wealth.

I envision a world where money serves Soul Purpose instead of acting as a deterrent or obstacle.

I envision a world where business owners invest in alignment with their Soul Purpose and make money from that purpose.

I envision a world where money is no longer the primary reason or excuse for people to do or not do something.

I envision a world where money is put in its proper role as a by-product of value and purpose.

PURPOSE

Live a life you love and create a legacy that lasts. Create a life you don't want to retire from and do things that fulfill you. By eliminating confusion and creating clarity around the philosophies and frameworks that lead to prosperity, we are no longer held captive to false and limiting beliefs.

Soul Purpose can now be the main focus in my family's life. Investing becomes aligned with Soul Purpose to bring forth even more wealth and energy for everyone.

A life of freedom and passion is made by deepening abilities and growing expertise, especially when fears about money are removed. When we are free to choose, a life well-lived leads to improved relationships and health.

By becoming financially independent, you can work because you want to, never because you have to in the name of making money. When money is no longer the primary reason or excuse for doing (or not doing) something, value and mission become the drivers. With stability and security, your thoughts can focus on happiness, creativity, and fulfillment. Being financially independent allows you to be a leader, especially in times of crisis.

When money is not the primary concern, the other areas of wealth can be given attention. Health is wealth. Purpose is wealth. The very mindset of value creation and service becomes wealth. This creates conditions where peace of mind, confidence, and growth are possible.

STRATEGY

Keep life simple financially. There are no such things as good investments, just good people with the right philosophies and the discipline to adhere to their philosophies, so always know who's behind the investment.

Read about marketing, communication, and human behavior, and continue to study through your preferred methods of learning. This could be through mastermind groups, study clubs, books, courses, or anything that assists you in enhancing and honing your skills.

Always have mentors. Work with people you love, trust, and enjoy; people committed to their Soul Purpose who support you in creating impact and value. Remove toxic people from your life and reserve that time for those who challenge you in a positive way. Find co-creators and collaborate rather than operate as a rugged individualist trying to compete in the hustle and grind.

Invest in multiplier relationships that bring out your best and that see and stand for the best version of you.

Investments aren't only about numbers and dollars; build mental and relationship capital.

A primary investment strategy is to impact the right people and create ways to more deeply impact them.

Always have contracts and agreements before moving forward on an investment and have great attorneys who can generate and review those contracts.

Before you invest, consider the impact on all other areas of your life. Manage your time wisely. Before you allocate time to a project or business, ask yourself if you can move forward without sacrificing your health, time with your family, or time for yourself.

Leisure is a worthwhile activity. Invest in hobbies and healthy habits where you can find time to listen to yourself and design the life that you love.

Make sure you have clean accounting books, review weekly reports and income statements, and keep separate accounts to store money for yourself.

When you do things in your business that others would normally be paid for, pay yourself for it.

Later in my Family Constitution, I share thoughts about living an intellectual life. Other sections are about health and fitness, personal character, quality of life, and even parenting. Here are some excerpts from those sections:

If you feed your mind with the most powerful thoughts through study, meditation, and connection to your source, great things will inevitably happen. Passion is the fuel for intellect and experience is a superior way to learn. Worry is the enemy of intellect. Questions are the gateway to intellect. Curiosity and openness lead to deeper understanding. Simplicity is organized intelligence. Energy flows where attention goes.

Engage in conversations that create conditions for growth, brainstorming, and wealth creation.

Create an environment where people bring their best and live to their highest potential for value creation.

At least monthly, travel somewhere or host someone at your house who is intellectually engaging and stimulating, allowing you to expand your knowledge.

Create an intention in conversation to be powerful and memorable, as if it is your only opportunity to talk with someone and you will be remembered by the conversation.

Interview people regularly. Do interviews to stay sharp and inventive, and invite the best speaker at an event to stay at your house to further the conversation and build more wealth.

Here are some questions to use to get to know someone.

- What's the single greatest lesson you've learned in your life?
- If you could have a conversation with yourself ten years ago, knowing what you know now, what would you say?
- What are the most important things in your life and business?
- What are the things that work in your life and why do they work?
- What are you reading?
- Whom have you studied?
- Who are your mentors?
- What are your daily rituals that lead to success?

When you invite people to dinner or your home and show up with intention, you get to learn the best of what they offer. Instead of trying to get their money, tap into their knowledge and information by adding value first.

Being healthy and active increases performance as a way to feel better in all areas of life. Health is foundational to success in all areas of life. When health is working, it can generate more energy and conditions for creativity and be a sign that all areas of life are working.

A healthy body creates space for a healthy mind. Health supports abundant thinking and removes self-doubt and self-conscious, negative thinking, allowing for the space to think clearly.

Exercise is the key to investing in oneself and therefore expanding one's energy and expression of Soul Purpose.

I have no control over my chronological age, but I can exercise a tremendous amount of control over my biological age. I can choose action that will improve my body and cause it to look and feel younger.

Character is a muscle that must be exercised to be consistent in all existence and reality. Character is consistent in an ever-changing external environment and comes from within. The eyes are the guiding beacon for character. Character must be consistent, especially in dealing with other people.

Character is a commitment. Money is easier to rebuild and restore than lost integrity.

You can never be less than 100% when it comes to commitment. Otherwise, it's just an interest. Without defined character and values, someone else's persuasiveness may lead one astray.

Integrity is gained by doing what you say you will do, or at minimum honoring your word by communicating and making a request to the other person to invent new possibilities or new timelines. The most powerful times to demonstrate integrity are when it's difficult, when it stretches you, or when you don't feel like handling it.

Enjoy great restaurants and great places, and experience the world in fine hotels and extravagant cities as a way to enjoy the fruits of your labor.

Be a steward of your possessions. Therefore, do not have so much that it ties or weighs you down. It's not necessary to own something to experience it. You can rent, borrow, or share with others. And that way, you can just buy the things that are extraordinarily important to you.

Quality of life is enhanced by going on trips. As a by-product, they advance our business because we're spending time with the movers and shakers of the world.

Work with clients and people who also become friends: those who appreciate what you do for them and implement with you to get the best results in their lives. These are the organizers, connectors, and initiators. They love our family and become some of our best friends.

As a parent, I teach my children to live in this world by believing in love. I want them to see the value in serving others, including those who are less fortunate than themselves. I want them to be brave and take chances on themselves. I want them to believe in their abilities to achieve anything they work toward. I want them to know how to solve problems on their own—and where to turn when they're lost. I want them to know that they can come to us for guidance and with questions. I want them to understand that they only get one body, so they should take good care of it. I want them to play big in life.

This is what legacy means to me.

As you read this, remember: progress over perfection. Life is filled with lessons, but we can guide our lives by being intentional. We can create resilience by sharing our tough times and find joy by celebrating the good ones. The conversations we have—and don't have—will be key to our legacies. Knowing stories about our families, where there was struggle and it required resilience and support, can massively impact our heirs.

It is time for you to create your own Family Constitution. We provide a guide that will ask you the necessary questions and give you the framework to outline what matters most for you and your legacy. Get your Legacy Builder free course now at rockefellersbook.com/legacy.

Designing your Family Constitution is not a one-time activity. Maybe just keep a journal with you at all times. Sometimes I send myself texts in the moment as a way to capture ideas. It doesn't have to be perfect. If your descendants expect perfection from you, they expect too much.

Just as with money, with a Family Constitution your heirs are not starting at zero. A family trust isn't just about leaving money behind; the Vanderbilt family proved that that's not enough. A family trust is also about leaving behind values, traditions, and knowledge that will carry on for generations. What you leave behind in your Family Constitution is bound to be read for generations to come, regardless of how much money you leave behind.

I don't know what the future has in store for us all. So there is wisdom in trusting your heirs to make good decisions utilizing the intellectual legacy you leave behind with the Family Constitution and board of trustees.

Start living your life more fully today. Start now, knowing that you have a framework for securing your most precious asset: your family. Use this formula as a gift of love to your family for generations to come.

Start by getting the free Legacy Builder course at rockefellersbook.com/legacy. Make space to work on it a little bit at a time. Then set up your trust and optimally funded whole life.

Progress over perfection, and done is better than perfect. Real is better than polished, and vulnerability is the key to connection. You don't get a second chance to create a legacy and live a life that you love.

The Economic Value of Certainty

It's a dark, frigid December night of sub-zero temperatures, and I'm driving through Wyoming on I-80 East. It feels like the middle of the night, but is barely after 8:00 p.m.

My girlfriend Carrie and I are running late getting to Green River, Wyoming, where we plan to meet up with my uncles for a trip to Jackson Hole.

I'm a slow driver; Carrie says I'm like an old man behind the wheel. This is a residual impact of getting in trouble with my mom for speeding tickets when I was a teenager. Still worried about getting a speeding ticket, I am pushing my own limits by setting the cruise control at eighty in a seventy-five zone—what a rebel. Yeah, Carrie was right to tease me.

I look around and see snow everywhere except for on the road ahead, which looks polished black and shiny. Concerned that it's black ice, I lightly touch the brakes to kill the cruise control.

The car immediately loses control and spins. It is like being on a carousel. Heart pounding, hands shaking, palms sweating, I throw my arm over Carrie. "Hold on, we are going to roll!" I shout.

Everything feels like it is happening in slow motion.

We spin around two-and-a-half times. And then we are sliding backward with the nose of our car facing the grille of a diesel truck—at eighty miles per hour.

"Brace yourself," I say as I start to turn the wheel.

We start spinning again, sliding across the ice and snow and down into the median. We slide almost all the way back up the median and nearly into oncoming traffic. And then finally, we stop.

We both sit in shock, staring forward and breathing heavily. Reality sets in. We. Are. Lucky.

A few hundred more feet forward and we'd have crashed into a concrete barrier. The only reason we didn't roll is because the road is solid ice. And even though we feel relieved to a degree, we are now afraid. Should we continue on?

I get out and look at the car. The bumper is packed with snow from the median, with weeds hanging out of the snowpack. The closest city is Green River, so after taking several deep breaths and embracing each other, we finally forge ahead.

If Carrie thought I drove too slow before, well, she is on the same page with me now.

I test just how slow a car could go on I-80. Five, maybe ten miles per hour. We are passed by car after car. Do they not know the risks? And now they are putting us at risk. Time slows. It is excruciating and frightening.

We finally arrive at my uncle's house, where they are debating over whether to leave us. I give my Uncle Drake the keys to my car because I am too shaken to drive any further.

His wife and daughter get in the car with us and my Uncle Page and his girlfriend drive off in his truck.

I recount the terror of our drive and things immediately get worse—Uncle Drake decides to tell us about his close calls, too, even looking back at us as he does this.

HEY! WATCH THE ROAD!!! My heart is pounding. I can see Carrie's heartbeat through her neck and she is grabbing my hand the same way she did later in our life when she was in labor with our first son. And now the terrain is even worse. We worry about the cliffs, much steeper than anything we saw on the drive to Green River. And now I am not in control.

As my uncle drives, I am afraid to speak up. Fear controls my every thought and emotion for the rest of the drive. Just before Jackson, we even see a bus crashed into a snowbank. But it does nothing to slow him down.

AVOID FINANCIAL "BLACK ICE"

I was triggered by my experience because the icy road was a blind spot. It was a risk. Where is the black ice in your finances, the blind spots and risks that jeopardize your legacy?

When we are young and don't know any better about money, it is easy to be seduced by risk: Like crypto gains. Like real estate appreciation and bidding to get properties—like bull markets with stocks. We take risks because we fall prey to greed, feeling like we are missing out. Or we think everyone else is doing it, so why shouldn't we?

But when we hit financial black ice, things change. People move to cash. They swear off investing. It is almost like when I drank in my twenties; I never understood the consequences until I went too far and had to throw up, swearing it off forever. But forever meant only until I forgot the pain.

These are the ebbs and flows of investing. Fear and greed. Ups and downs. Forgetting and making mistakes after time passes.

When I hit that black ice, there was no more joy, the trip was no longer fun, and I wasn't dreaming about Jackson Hole any longer. I was just trying to survive.

This is what happens when people lose money and don't utilize the Rockefeller Method or understand their Investor DNA to become better investors. This is why it is so dangerous to chase returns without a plan or without protecting the downside. Risk and ignorance destroy dreams, lives, and legacy. Poor philosophy invites fear and creates loss.

Most people live in fear, worry, and survival mode every day. Paycheck to paycheck. Bill after bill. *Where will the money come from? What can be done to gain safety and security? Should I work harder? Sacrifice more?*

This is how most of the human race operates. In fear. In scarcity. Scarred from past experience, their version of barely getting out alive. A tough economy, career change, bankruptcy, market losses: These are the financial "black ice" moments in life.

The scarcity mindset leads people to believe in a zero-sum, winner-takes-all world of taking what you can and holding onto whatever you have. In this dangerous world, people are worried that they will make a mistake, worried that they are not enough, and simply worried.

Protection and preservation can prevent prosperity. The way I drove after hitting the ice was about protection and preservation. But if I had known about the conditions, or had contingencies or other options, things could have been different. Education and prevention are key.

What's the difference between protection and preservation, and education and prevention?

They are reactive versus proactive, for one. When we play not to lose, we live in fear and are governed by scarcity. When we utilize education and take precautions, we can remain present, and with certainty comes the possibility of being present.

We are all in store for financial surprises. Yet with the proper planning, 90% or more of those surprises do not have to derail us at all and will not destroy our lives, finances, legacy, or enjoyment.

There is an economic value to certainty. If I'd been certain the roads were clear and safe, I could have driven without fear and made more progress. But being caught off guard and feeling blindsided created a new reality of concern. On the other hand, if I had known the roads were icy, I could have prevented spinning and feeling out of control. I could have chosen a different path. Driving during the day. Flying. Having studded snow tires on the car.

The Rockefeller Method is about creating certainty. It is about having the most options with the least risk through coordination, planning, and risk management.

Where do past financial blind spots (aka "black ice") impact your life? Do you feel behind? Are you unclear about your financial risks? Are you exposed due to a lack of asset protection, trust planning, and insurance coverage to transfer risk? Do you worry that you don't have enough savings and liquidity to handle a career change, economic turmoil, or a health challenge? Are you concerned that your investments might not perform or are still judging yourself for past mistakes?

If you answered yes to any of these questions, there is a high likelihood that money concerns and worry are creating stress and running in the background of your thoughts, slowing you down and robbing you of peace of mind and joy. This is why the Rockefeller Method is so instrumental and foundational.

They say ignorance is bliss, but it leads to risk. There is an economic value to certainty and to knowing what you can count on.

Who in your life can alert you to your blind spots? Do you have an awareness of what is working or not working in your financial life? How will you gain the knowledge that will illuminate the truth of your financial matters?

In today's economy, there is plenty of "black ice": inflation (through quantitative easing and fractionalized banking), tax changes, interest fluctuations, insurance structure and asset protection, investment fees, and risk. Awareness is key to avoiding the black ice before you spin.

Here are the top five things you can do to create certainty, therefore increasing abundance, removing blind spots, and allowing you to swing for the fences in your life:

1. **Create Financial Independence:** This means you have enough cash flow from your assets to cover expenses.

2. **Protect Your Downside:** Set up an asset protection trust or family trust and focus on risk management and mitigation to keep more

of what you have invested.

3. **Plug Financial Leaks:** Utilize the four I's of efficiency: IRS, interest, investments, and insurance. Stop overpaying on tax and interest, detect and remove hidden fees and commissions that come with investments, and remove duplicate coverages and improper policy design in your insurance.

4. **Build a Peace of Mind Fund:** Create enough savings in your optimally funded whole life to take advantage of opportunities and create peace of mind.

5. **Increase Your Financial Literacy:** Do everything you can to continue increasing your financial literacy, getting your free Legacy Builder course at rockefellersbook.com/legacy..

These five guidelines are like guardrails protecting you from financial danger.

It is time to create certainty in your life and feel confident in your direction. Without this certainty, risk will reign and fear will confiscate your time and wealth. Having a solid foundation provides you with the economic value of certainty. When you have predictability, when you know exactly what the guaranteed standards of performance are, you can make decisions with a lot more peace of mind and confidence. You have less stress, you lose less sleep, and you don't have to watch your emotions follow your money when the market goes down.

If you have a policy in which the cost of insurance can change, as in universal life policies, or the company can ask you to pay a higher premium in the future, or your earnings are completely dependent upon what happens in the stock market, you don't have that certainty. Those are the financial black ice spots that destroy wealth and confidence.

When people have money stress and are limited by misinformation, mishaps, and myths that lead them astray, it causes damage to relationships and creates conditions that can lead to frustration within the family, and even to divorce.

If your financial foundation is built upon hype, hope, or risk, your legacy suffers. A war chest or opportunity fund cannot be dependent on factors outside of your control, like higher insurance costs, downturns in the market, etc. It must be available when it is time to use it.

The cash value of a whole life policy is both accessible and guaranteed. You know for certain, year by year, how much money will be there. That certainty can be leveraged in all areas of your life, especially as you make short- and long-term financial decisions. Whole life insurance allows you to lay a solid foundation so you can swing for the fences and still protect your family's quality of life, Rockefeller style.

This is the map that creates predictable success and sustainable wealth for future generations.

How "Buy Term and Invest the Difference" Stacks Up Against Optimally Funded Whole Life

Imagine that you buy term life insurance now and invest the difference in a qualified retirement plan, mutual fund, or anything else. When you retire at some future date, you end up with a certain amount of money to live off.

Let's assume that at age sixty-five, you have $4 million in your retirement account. Thinking that you're now "self-insured," you cancel your term insurance. You can transfer your $4 million net worth to your spouse or other beneficiaries.

Meanwhile, let's say your $4 million is earning 5% interest. Because you want to preserve your wealth for and transfer it to your heirs, or simply because you don't know how long you'll live, you only live off the interest. At 5%, that interest comes to $200,000 per year. However, after taxes of $36,042, you're actually left with $163,958 per year for your retirement income.

This is a generous assumption, because where can you find a secure investment that pays a steady 5% annually? For the sake of illustration, we'll keep it generous.

Consider the following illustrations, generated by the Truth Concepts calculator created by Todd Langford, which show how this strategy stacks up against whole life.

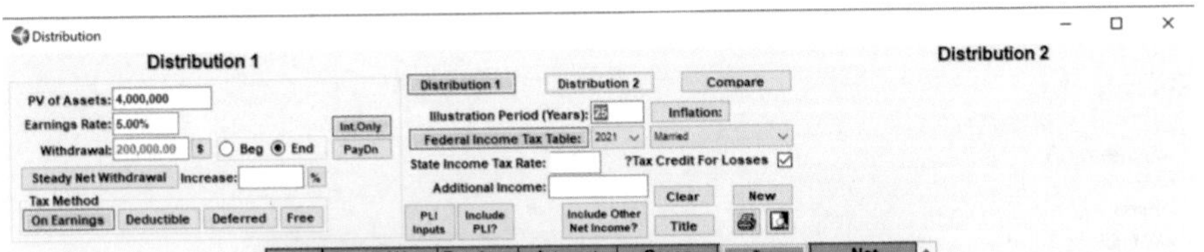

YEAR	Beg. Of Year Acct. Value	Earnings Rate	Interest Earnings	Gross Withdrawal	Tax Payment	Net Spendable
1	4,000,000	5.00%	200,000	(200,000)	(36,042)	163,958
2	4,000,000	5.00%	200,000	(200,000)	(36,042)	163,958
3	4,000,000	5.00%	200,000	(200,000)	(36,042)	163,958
4	4,000,000	5.00%	200,000	(200,000)	(36,042)	163,958
5	4,000,000	5.00%	200,000	(200,000)	(36,042)	163,958
6	4,000,000	5.00%	200,000	(200,000)	(36,042)	163,958
7	4,000,000	5.00%	200,000	(200,000)	(36,042)	163,958
8	4,000,000	5.00%	200,000	(200,000)	(36,042)	163,958
9	4,000,000	5.00%	200,000	(200,000)	(36,042)	163,958
10	4,000,000	5.00%	200,000	(200,000)	(36,042)	163,958
11	4,000,000	5.00%	200,000	(200,000)	(36,042)	163,958
12	4,000,000	5.00%	200,000	(200,000)	(36,042)	163,958
13	4,000,000	5.00%	200,000	(200,000)	(36,042)	163,958
14	4,000,000	5.00%	200,000	(200,000)	(36,042)	163,958
15	4,000,000	5.00%	200,000	(200,000)	(36,042)	163,958
16	4,000,000	5.00%	200,000	(200,000)	(36,042)	163,958
17	4,000,000	5.00%	200,000	(200,000)	(36,042)	163,958
18	4,000,000	5.00%	200,000	(200,000)	(36,042)	163,958
19	4,000,000	5.00%	200,000	(200,000)	(36,042)	163,958
20	4,000,000	5.00%	200,000	(200,000)	(36,042)	163,958
TOTAL	4,000,000	5.00%	5,000,000	5,000,000	(901,044)	4,098,956

Illustration 1

When you don't have any life insurance in your retirement, your assets become your life insurance. Living on interest only leaves people susceptible to a scarcity mindset. Since the number one fear of retirees is running out of money, you're taught to never touch your $4 million principal. Ultimately, that $4 million goes to your beneficiaries, and you never used any of it.

Moreover, there's another problem with this scenario: Interest rates have been extraordinarily low and volatile investments are even worse. Where do you put your money to safely get that return? Where would Dave Ramsey and Suze Orman say to get it? I certainly don't know of an easy place to do that outside of whole life insurance policy dividends and annuities, which are also life insurance products.

Let's be slightly more realistic and say you buy term and invest the difference, and that leaves you earning 3% interest on your principal. After tax, that puts your yearly income at $102,103. So you're worth $4 million, but only spending $102,103 per year for fear of spending down your principal and running out of money. Does that seem right to you? (See Illustration 2.)

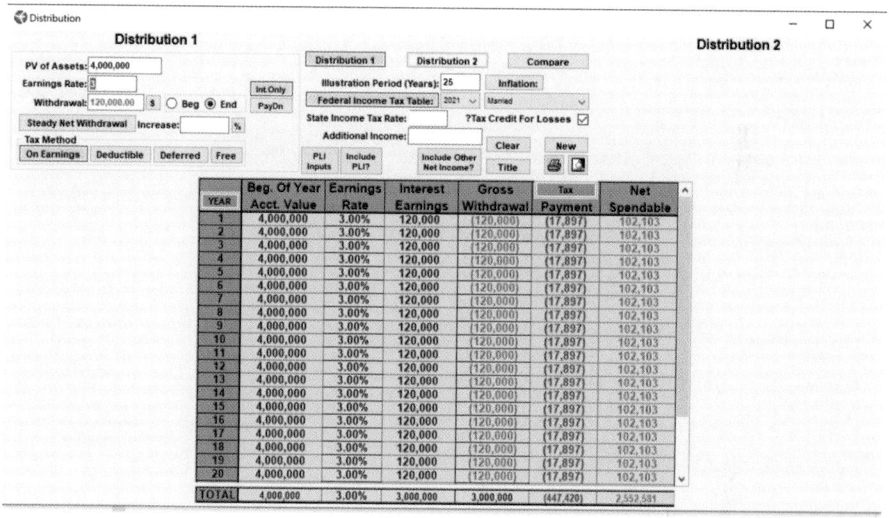

YEAR	Beg. Of Year Acct. Value	Earnings Rate	Interest Earnings	Gross Withdrawal	Tax Payment	Net Spendable
1	4,000,000	3.00%	120,000	(120,000)	(17,897)	102,103
2	4,000,000	3.00%	120,000	(120,000)	(17,897)	102,103
3	4,000,000	3.00%	120,000	(120,000)	(17,897)	102,103
4	4,000,000	3.00%	120,000	(120,000)	(17,897)	102,103
5	4,000,000	3.00%	120,000	(120,000)	(17,897)	102,103
6	4,000,000	3.00%	120,000	(120,000)	(17,897)	102,103
7	4,000,000	3.00%	120,000	(120,000)	(17,897)	102,103
8	4,000,000	3.00%	120,000	(120,000)	(17,897)	102,103
9	4,000,000	3.00%	120,000	(120,000)	(17,897)	102,103
10	4,000,000	3.00%	120,000	(120,000)	(17,897)	102,103
11	4,000,000	3.00%	120,000	(120,000)	(17,897)	102,103
12	4,000,000	3.00%	120,000	(120,000)	(17,897)	102,103
13	4,000,000	3.00%	120,000	(120,000)	(17,897)	102,103
14	4,000,000	3.00%	120,000	(120,000)	(17,897)	102,103
15	4,000,000	3.00%	120,000	(120,000)	(17,897)	102,103
16	4,000,000	3.00%	120,000	(120,000)	(17,897)	102,103
17	4,000,000	3.00%	120,000	(120,000)	(17,897)	102,103
18	4,000,000	3.00%	120,000	(120,000)	(17,897)	102,103
19	4,000,000	3.00%	120,000	(120,000)	(17,897)	102,103
20	4,000,000	3.00%	120,000	(120,000)	(17,897)	102,103
TOTAL	4,000,000	3.00%	3,000,000	3,000,000	(447,420)	2,552,581

Illustration 2

The truth is, that was the plan for the financial institutions anyway. Remember the four rules of financial institutions? They want your money, as often as possible, hold onto it as long as possible and give you back the least possible. How's that "long-haul" investment plan you were sold decades ago looking now?

Now let's consider a different scenario using whole life insurance and investing the difference utilizing the cash value. We'll assume that by the age of sixty-five, you end up with the same amount—$4 million—in your cash value for retirement. Except now, you have both the $4 million in cash value *and* a $4 million death benefit.

What does this mean for you? It means you now have a permission slip to spend your $4 million—because you have a guaranteed $4 million also going to your beneficiaries in the form of a death benefit, no matter what. You are no longer held captive to living off your interest alone. When you die, your death benefit will replace whatever money you've spent while you were alive for your heirs. So now, instead of just spending interest, you get to spend both the interest and the principal in your retirement years. And what if you live past the twenty years we used in these examples? You have a large death benefit that you can use to create more income as we discussed throughout this book.

Let's look at this more closely and do the math. Assuming a 3% interest rate and paying down your principal to zero over twenty-five years, you'll be able to spend $211,815 in the first year. That's over 50% above the $102,103 in the last scenario! (See Example 3.)

Let's take it even further. Let's put Example 1 back at 5% and leave Example 2 at 3% interest. In Example 1, you get $163,958 per year. With whole life, Example 2 still gives you a whole lot more! Even if we take Example 1 down to 2% interest, you still get $195,680 in your first year. And how about 1% interest? That's $177,225. (See Example 4.)

YEAR	Beg. Of Year Acct. Value	Earnings Rate	Gross Withdrawal	Tax Payment	Net Spendable	Beg. Of Year Acct. Value	Earnings Rate	Gross Withdrawal	Tax Payment	Net Spendable
1	4,000,000	5.00%	(200,000)	(36,042)	163,958	4,000,000	1.00%	(181,627)	(4,402)	177,225
2	4,000,000	5.00%	(200,000)	(36,042)	163,958	3,858,373	1.00%	(181,627)	(4,232)	177,395
3	4,000,000	5.00%	(200,000)	(36,042)	163,958	3,715,330	1.00%	(181,627)	(4,060)	177,567
4	4,000,000	5.00%	(200,000)	(36,042)	163,958	3,570,856	1.00%	(181,627)	(3,887)	177,740
5	4,000,000	5.00%	(200,000)	(36,042)	163,958	3,424,938	1.00%	(181,627)	(3,712)	177,915
6	4,000,000	5.00%	(200,000)	(36,042)	163,958	3,277,560	1.00%	(181,627)	(3,535)	178,092
7	4,000,000	5.00%	(200,000)	(36,042)	163,958	3,128,708	1.00%	(181,627)	(3,356)	178,271
8	4,000,000	5.00%	(200,000)	(36,042)	163,958	2,978,369	1.00%	(181,627)	(3,176)	178,451
9	4,000,000	5.00%	(200,000)	(36,042)	163,958	2,826,525	1.00%	(181,627)	(2,994)	178,633
10	4,000,000	5.00%	(200,000)	(36,042)	163,958	2,673,163	1.00%	(181,627)	(2,810)	178,817
11	4,000,000	5.00%	(200,000)	(36,042)	163,958	2,518,268	1.00%	(181,627)	(2,624)	179,003
12	4,000,000	5.00%	(200,000)	(36,042)	163,958	2,361,824	1.00%	(181,627)	(2,436)	179,191
13	4,000,000	5.00%	(200,000)	(36,042)	163,958	2,203,815	1.00%	(181,627)	(2,246)	179,381
14	4,000,000	5.00%	(200,000)	(36,042)	163,958	2,044,226	1.00%	(181,627)	(2,055)	179,572
15	4,000,000	5.00%	(200,000)	(36,042)	163,958	1,883,041	1.00%	(181,627)	(1,883)	179,744
16	4,000,000	5.00%	(200,000)	(36,042)	163,958	1,720,245	1.00%	(181,627)	(1,720)	179,907
17	4,000,000	5.00%	(200,000)	(36,042)	163,958	1,555,820	1.00%	(181,627)	(1,556)	180,071
18	4,000,000	5.00%	(200,000)	(36,042)	163,958	1,389,751	1.00%	(181,627)	(1,390)	180,237
19	4,000,000	5.00%	(200,000)	(36,042)	163,958	1,222,022	1.00%	(181,627)	(1,222)	180,405
20	4,000,000	5.00%	(200,000)	(36,042)	163,958	1,052,615	1.00%	(181,627)	(1,053)	180,574
TOTAL	4,000,000	5.00%	5,000,000	(901,844)	4,098,956	0	1.00%	4,540,675	(57,010)	4,483,665

With whole life insurance, you can earn as little as 1% interest on your cash value, but still be in a much better place than you would be if you'd bought term and invested the difference. (Of course, that's only assuming you found a safe investment that earns a steady 5% annually.)

You may currently be in a position where your cash flow isn't strong enough to allocate any extra money to permanent life insurance. If that's the case, there are term policies that can be converted into whole life policies in the future. So if you have to buy term insurance, make sure it's convertible and with a company you would want your properly structured, optimally funded whole life policy with when you convert it.

Get the Legacy Builder Course

The Legacy Builder Course is an immensely valuable tool in helping you to consciously and wisely start building your family and financial legacy. The course includes video instruction and a detailed forty-three-page workbook to support you in implementing everything you've learned in this book.

The course is broken up into the following three phases of legacy planning:

Phase I: How to Initiate a Lasting Family Legacy

In this section, you'll be guided to:

- Create your family trust.

- Involve your children in building a legacy, thereby ensuring their long-term productivity and success.

- "Keep the money together" by initiating the Rockefeller Method and setting up your financial structure properly.

- Start paying yourself first, automatically.

Phase II: The Family Constitution

In this section, I'll give you instructions on how to:

- Create a Family Constitution that prevents your heirs from getting spoiled and protects your legacy against such a possibility.
- Clearly define your family legacy so you have a thorough and clear vision of what you're building.
- Select the Board of Trustees for your family trust.

Phase III: Family Meetings and Retreats

This section gives you detailed support in learning how to:

- Set up family meetings to be as productive and beneficial as possible.
- Establish family values, rules, traditions, rituals, habits, and goals.
- Create your family crest, mantra, and creed.
- Teach your kids about money.

Get the course for free now at rockefellersbook.com/legacy.

End Notes

Chapter 1

1. https://www.celebritynetworth.com/articles/billionaire-news/updated-list-richest-americans-time/

2. https://economictimes.indiatimes.com/markets/stocks/news/lesson-from-vanderbilt-when-you-invest-you-gotta-do-the-leg-work/articleshow/69160454.cms?from=mdr

3. All details about the life of Cornelius Vanderbilt were taken from Wikipedia: https://en.wikipedia.org/wiki/Cornelius_Vanderbilt

4. https://en.wikipedia.org/wiki/Rockefeller_family

Chapter 3

1. https://www.forbes.com/profile/rockefeller/?sh=1d657881430e

2. https://www.archives.gov/founding-docs/constitution-q-and-a

3. https://www.forbes.com/sites/brianluster/2014/03/18/why-forming-a-family-limited-partnership-means-less-stress-at-tax-time/?sh=58f275c78658

Chapter 4

1. htktps://www.forbes.com/sites/kerryadolan/2020/12/17/billion-dollar-dynasties-these-are-the-richest-families-in-america/?sh=b155d83772c7

2. https://www.americanbanker.com/list/dramatic-collapses-made-2023-the-biggest-year-ever-for-bank-failures

3. https://www.insuranceandestates.com/life-insurance-creditor-protection-by-state/

Chapter 5

1. https://paradigmlife.net/5-businesses-saved-cash-value-life-insurance/

2. https://www.nytimes.com/1994/12/08/business/orange-county-s-bankruptcy-the-overview-orange-county-crisis-jolts-bond-market.html

3. https://www.reuters.com/article/idUSBREA4603A/

4. https://www.nytimes.com/2008/11/15/business/yourmoney/15money.html

5. https://www.thinkadvisor.com/2013/09/09/a-brief-history-of-life-insurance/

6. https://hbr.org/2015/03/how-life-insurers-can-bring-their-business-into-the-21st-century

Chapter 7

1. https://www.entrepreneur.com/money-finance/is-this-the-worst-financial-advice-ever/310731

Chapter 8

1. https://finance.yahoo.com/news/one-worst-financial-products-alive-103000138.html

2. https://www.policygenius.com/life-insurance/news/suze-orman-term-life-insurance-whole-life-insurance/

Chapter 11

1. https://www.linkedin.com/pulse/cold-math-investment-fees-how-2-annual-can-reduce-40-michael-h-/

2. https://truthconcepts.com/calculators/

Chapter 12

1. https://en.wikipedia.org/wiki/Bessemer_Trust

2. https://www.barrons.com/articles/SB125936529386967205

Chapter 13

1. https://www.mindvalley.com/lifebook